A TASTE OF ONTARIO COUNTRY INNS

A TASTE OF ONTARIO COUNTRY INNS

Copyright © 1991 by David Scott
Whitecap Books
Vancouver/Toronto

All rights reserved. No part of this publication may be reproduced, stored in a retrieval system or transmitted, in any form or by any means, electronic, mechanical, photocopying, recording or otherwise, without prior written permission of the publisher.

Edited by Shaun Oakey
Cover photograph by Thomas Kitchin/First Light
Cover and interior design by Carolyn Deby

Interior illustrations signed W. Reid by Wendy Reid. All other interior illustrations used with permission of individual inns.

Typography by CompuType, Vancouver, B.C.

Printed and bound in Canada by D.W. Friesen and Sons Ltd.

Canadian Cataloguing in Publication Data

Scott, David, 1939-
   A taste of Ontario country inns

   Includes index.
   ISBN 1-895099-95-1

   1. Hotels, taverns, etc.—Ontario—Guide-books.
2. Restaurants, lunch rooms, etc.—Ontario
—Guide-books. I. Title.
TX907.5.C22O56 1991   647.94713′01   C91-091476-1

To my friend Jan Gardiner,
publisher of *Inn Business Magazine*,
who inspired this book
over dim sum in Bangkok
between the ice cube and Bufferin courses

CONTENTS

Introduction ix
Inn Rates xi
The Towns
   Alliston 1
   Alton 4
   Amherstburg 10
   Ancaster 12
   Bayfield 15
   Beachburg 21
   Benmiller—*see Goderich*
   Bloomfield 23
   Bracebridge 29
   Cambridge 32
   Cataract—*see Alton*
   Chaffey's Locks 38
   Cobourg 41
   Collingwood 44
   Combermere 46
   Dryden 48
   Elgin—*see Chaffey's Locks*
   Elmira 50
   Elora 53
   Emo 56
   Exeter 58

Goderich	61
Heidelberg	70
Huntsville	72
Ingersoll	78
Kingston	81
Kitchener	83
Manitoulin Island—*see Spring Bay*	
Meaford	86
Milton	88
Mount Pleasant	90
New Dundee	92
New Hamburg	95
Niagara-on-the-Lake	98
North Bay	104
Ottawa	106
Pelee Island	109
Port Dover	111
Port Elgin	114
Port Stanley	116
Rossport	119
Sault Ste. Marie	122
Severn Bridge	126
Shelburne	129
St. Jacobs	132
South Gillies	135
Southampton	138
Spring Bay	141
Stittsville	144
Stratford	147
Thunder Bay—*see South Gillies*	
Trout Creek	150
Violet Hill—*see Shelburne*	
Walkerton	152
Williamsford	155
Wolfe Island	157
Zurich	160
Index of the Inns	163
Index of the Recipes	164

INTRODUCTION

The inns described in this book are just a taste of what is available throughout this enormous province. There were so many delightful inns to choose from, I had a difficult time deciding which ones to include in this sampling and I only hope I didn't exclude your personal favorite!

All of the entries I chose offer a peaceful oasis where the wayfarer can break his journey and dine superbly in relaxing surroundings. Some of them also offer accommodations for overnight guests.

A few of these inns were built for that purpose a century or more ago; others have been cleverly wrought from ancient mills or other buildings whose original function has long been overtaken by technology. Some have only been operating for a few years but have already succeeded in providing the quality and ambience that merit their inclusion. It's wonderful to see historic buildings earning their preservation through their new owners' ingenuity and having the loving care lavished on them now that few enjoyed during their first century of service.

Many of the inns are physical extensions of the owner's personality, the menu often a legacy of his ethnic origin, travels, or special interests. Innkeepers are a very special breed and, if you can catch them for a chat during their very limited free time, you will find that most have interesting experiences to recall and all have observations on the state of the nation.

I would also like to assure you that no payment of any kind was accepted from any of the inns I chose to list. Indeed, most innkeepers were not aware of what I was doing until my surprise inspection was completed and I introduced myself in order to gather additional information.

Ontario has hundreds of wonderful inns, and I sincerely hope you enjoy visiting the very special places described in this book as much as I did while researching them.

INN RATES

Lunch and Dinner

$ under $10
$$ $10–$20
$$$ $20–$30
$$$$ $30–$40
$$$$$ $40–$50
$$$$$$ more than $50

The dollar symbols reflect the average cost of a meal for one person without drinks and before taxes.

Accommodation, double occupancy

$ under $50
$$ $50–$70
$$$ $70–$90
$$$$ $90–$110
$$$$$ $110–$120
$$$$$$ more than $120

The dollar symbols reflect each inn's lowest-priced double room. Room rates may vary widely.

Nottawasaga Inn

A full-service, four-star country retreat in Toronto's back yard, with seminar facilities, fine dining, golf, indoor and outdoor pools and all the exercise toys.

Innkeeper:	Lou Biffis
Address:	P.O. Box 1110, Alliston, Ont. L0M 1A0
Telephone:	705-435-5501
Rooms:	165 rooms and suites all with bathroom en suite
Children:	Yes
Pets:	No
Open:	Year round
Room rates:	$$$$. Off-season packages available
Food rates:	Lunch $; Dinner $$
Smoking:	No restrictions; no-smoking dining areas
Dress code:	Jacket preferred in dining room
Facilities:	18-hole, par-70 golf course; 18-hole miniature golf course; driving range; pro shop; fitness center; indoor and outdoor swimming pools; racquetball courts; sauna; whirlpool; video arcade; volleyball; soccer; horseshoe pits; cross-country skiing; skating; lounge; café restaurant; 2 dining rooms; gift shop; 31 meetings rooms; 4 boardrooms; meeting facilities for up to 2,000
Attractions:	Near Barrie Raceway; Base Borden Military Museum; Molson Park; Gryphon Theatre; Simcoe County Museum and Archives; Centennial Beach Park; Sharon Temple
Wheelchairs:	All public rooms and guest rooms accessible
Directions:	On Highway 89, 3 km (2 miles) west of Highway 400 or 3 km (2 miles) east of Alliston, about 60 km (37 miles) northwest of Toronto

The brochure says the Nottawasaga Inn offers "city style amenities in a relaxing country atmosphere," and that's precisely what you get at this well-planned, self-contained resort. It's the sort of place where you forget about your car until it's time to leave because there's plenty to keep you busy — or just lazing around — until it's time to go home.

Innkeeper Lou Biffis built the resort in 1965 after beating the bushes for voters to help him win a liquor plebiscite in Tecumseth Township, which had been dry for 58 years. In 1987 a major expansion more than doubled the number of rooms and increased the meeting and sporting facilities.

The inn makes no bones about catering to corporate think tanks and their ubiquitous meetings. But seeing the participants scurrying off to sessions with their briefcases and clipboards on a beautiful day somehow gives the vacationer's schedule of idolatry a sharper edge. It's a bit like having a Monday off and watching everybody else going to work.

Accommodation runs from standard rooms, which are large, to suites with whirlpools and king-size beds. The standard rooms have two double beds, desk space (for those who have homework from their meetings!), table and two chairs and four-piece bathrooms.

If you're booking a standard room, be sure to specify you want one of those facing west across the river and golf course instead of one of the 45 that overlook a blacktopped parking lot. Many of the west-facing rooms have access to a large sun deck and the outdoor pool; those on the second floor have balconies overlooking the pool area and sun deck.

Light meals are available through the day and evening at The Inn Café, which offers finger foods, snacks, salads and super sandwiches fully garnished, and standard North American entrees.

The Riverview Dining Room is less formal than the Mahogany Room and generally offers lighter entrees — fish, pastas, a vegetable dish, brochettes and stir-fry, though there is prime rib, rack of lamb, chicken and four steaks.

The Mahogany Room, named for its paneling and furniture, is designed for those special dining experiences, with dishes like beef Wellington, salmon fillet stuffed with scallop mousse and poached in a white wine sauce, sautéed veal medallions topped with crab meat and asparagus and glazed with sauce Béarnaise . . .

Chef Phil Houghtling is a Canadian who trained in Canada and Europe and has worked in Europe and the U.S., winning awards along the way for buffet presentations, ice carvings and tallow sculptures. Phil has made available one of his recipes, which is popular with guests at the inn.

Nottawasaga Inn White/dark Chocolate Mousse
(Serves 6)

To make dark mousse use dark chocolate; to make white mousse, use white chocolate. The following recipe is for dark mousse.

6 oz dark chocolate
2 egg yolks
1/3 cup sugar
1/3 cup unsalted butter
2 oz Kahlua
1 cup 35% cream
2 egg whites
6 whole strawberries for garnish

In a medium bowl over a pan of hot water, melt chocolate until smooth. In a small bowl, whip egg yolks and sugar over hot water with a wire whisk until pale yellow. Slowly whip melted butter into yolks. Add Kahlua; remove from heat. Pour melted chocolate into egg mixture, stirring with a clean whisk until smooth. Cool. Whip cream until stiff. Whip egg whites until stiff. Fold whipped cream into chocolate mixture. Fold in egg whites until smooth. Pour into six champagne glasses or dessert glasses in layers, or half and half. Garnish with whipped cream and a strawberry. Refrigerate before serving.

Cataract Inn

A small, recently refurbished country inn that has been operating in the Caledon Hills northwest of Toronto since 1855 and earning a reputation for fine cuisine.

Innkeepers:	Rodney and Jennifer Hough
Address:	R.R. 2, Alton, Ont. L0N 1A0
Telephone:	519-927-3033
Rooms:	5 rooms, shared bathrooms
Children:	No facilities
Pets:	No
Open:	Year round. Lunch, Fri.-Sun. noon-3; Dinner, daily 5:30-10. Dining room closed Tuesdays Jan. through May. Closed Christmas
Room rates:	$$, including continental breakfast
Food rates:	Lunch $; Dinner $$
Smoking:	In designated areas
Dress code:	Semi-casual; prefer no jeans at dinner
Attractions:	On the Bruce Trail; near alpine and cross-country skiing
Wheelchairs:	Dining room and patio accessible
Directions:	In the hamlet of Cataract, 18 km (11 miles) south of Orangeville on Highway 136. Turn on the 3rd Line west of Caledon 1 km (1/2 mile) south of Highways 24 and 136.

Rodney and Jennifer Hough offer what Rodney calls "short-term relief valves" at their postcard-perfect historic inn in the Caledon Hills. They believe their guests come to Cataract and the Cataract Inn so they can get away from the noise of cities and the hassles of careers.

So the red-brick inn with crisp white trim is the ideal retreat for rest and relaxation. The rooms don't have television sets or telephones and breakfast is served when you decide to get out of bed and wander downstairs for it.

The large guest rooms have different configurations and different views of the woods and farm fields of the Caledon Hills. The inn sits high on the banks of the cedar-lined Credit River just across the road from the 975-acre Credit Provincial Park.

Rooms are furnished with antiques, decorated with restful paints and wallpapers, and all the paintings hanging on the walls have recently been replaced. "The ones we had before were sort of cold," Rodney explains. "The ones we have now make the rooms more cozy." And so do the fluffy terrycloth robes hanging on pegs on the backs of the doors. Guests can use them for the short walk down the hall to the large common bathrooms.

The inn has three small licensed dining rooms and an outdoor patio for sipping and dining in summer. The menus are small, too, but have imaginative offerings to suit most palates. Fine food is the inn's métier, and the Houghs have developed a flourishing off-premises catering service for everything from weddings to corporate Christmas parties.

By arrangement, guests can take off into the park or countryside with a picnic basket full of goodies from the inn's kitchen . . . or take a hot-air balloon flight from the back yard.

Passersby can also drop in at the inn by prior arrangement and collect complete picnics from Gourmet To Go, another service of the inn.

Chef Tim O'Donnell has passed along a special recipe from the Cataract's menus.

Cataract Inn Raspberry Soufflé

(Serves 6)

10 oz frozen raspberries in light syrup, thawed
4 egg whites, room temperature
1/2 cup sugar
1 cup chilled 35% cream
1 oz raspberry liqueur

Preheat oven to 375° F. Butter 6 individual soufflé dishes and lightly coat with sugar. In a food processor or blender, process the raspberries in their syrup until smooth. In a bowl, beat the egg whites until they form soft peaks. Blend in the sugar, 1 T at a time, and continue beating until stiff and glossy. Fold in the raspberry purée. Pour the batter into the prepared dishes. Bake until lightly golden, 12–15 minutes.

While the soufflés are baking, whip the cream with the raspberry liqueur to soft peaks. Serve the soufflés hot from the oven, capped with the whipped cream.

The Millcroft Inn

A nineteenth-century stone knitting mill converted to an exquisite full-service country inn overlooking a millpond and pretty stream; one of Canada's finest hostelries.

Innkeeper:	Mark Harrison
Address:	P.O. Box 89, John St., Alton, Ont. L0N 1A0
Telephone:	519-941-8111
Rooms:	42 rooms and suites all with bathroom en suite
Children:	Yes
Pets:	No
Open:	Year round. Lunch noon–2:30; Dinner 6–9; Afternoon tea daily 2–5
Room rates:	$$$$$$ single or double occupancy
Food rates:	Lunch $$$; Dinner $$$$$$
Smoking:	No cigars or pipes in dining room. No smoking in dining pod
Dress code:	No jeans, please
Facilities:	Outdoor heated swimming pool, sauna, whirlpool, fireplaces and hot tubs in some rooms, tennis, horseback riding, nearby ballooning, hiking trails in 100 acres of the Caledon Hills
Attractions:	Boutiques, antique shops; near Orangeville's Dufferin County Museum; Brampton's Great War Flying Museum; Peel Heritage Complex; Wild Water Kingdom
Wheelchairs:	Patio, dining room and some guest rooms accessible

Directions: Take Highway 410 north from Highway 401. At the village of Caledon, turn left on Highway 24 and drive 5 km (3 miles) to Highway 136. Turn right and go 5 km (3 miles) to Alton. Turn left at the main crossroads, drive past a second stop sign and follow the signs into the Millcroft Inn.

The Millcroft Inn's membership in the prestigious Relais & Chateaux association succinctly explains a lot about the way this inn is operated. There are only 377 hotels and restaurants in 37 countries that so far meet the association's stringent quality-control criteria in the categories of character, courtesy, calm, comfort and cuisine.

Quite simply, The Millcroft is one of the world's finest inns. Any doubts the visitor may have are dispelled by just walking into the reception area of the four-story former mill, built in 1881. Two years of restoration work was carried out before The Millcroft Inn opened in 1977, and every care was taken to maintain the building's architectural integrity.

There are 22 guest rooms in the original mill building; across the creek is a complex called The Crofts, containing 20 units with fireplace in the sitting room, outdoor patio and an upstairs sleeping loft. Rooms in the mill are all air-conditioned and have a sitting area. There are dark wooden beams, pale pastel walls and rugs and a blend of European and Canadian antique furniture. Rooms in The Crofts are contemporary, with light wall colors, modern furniture and light and dark woods.

The timbered dining room overlooks falls from the millpond and Shaw's Creek. A glass-walled pod is cantilevered out from the dining room over the creek and has seating for a dozen people.

The dining room is a stage for the Millcroft's executive chef, Fredy Stamm. He changes the menus monthly, but with advance notice Stamm will prepare any guest's favorite dish. In summer the vegetables are from the inn's own gardens.

Stamm is the author of a well-known cookbook titled *Fredy Stamm, The Millcroft Inn*, and he has kindly consented to the use of the following recipe.

Millcroft Inn Braised Veal Shank à l'Orange

(Serves 6)

1 carrot
1 celery heart
1/2 onion
3 lbs veal shank
Salt, pepper, paprika
1/4 cup unsalted butter

10 juicy oranges
1 1/4 cups maple syrup
2/3 cup white wine
2/3 cup veal jus
1/3 cup vegetable broth

Preheat oven to 375° F.

Clean the vegetables and cut them into half-inch cubes. Trim the veal shank of excess fat and gristle; remove the membrane. Rub the shank lightly with salt, pepper and paprika. Melt the butter in a roasting pan over medium heat. Slowly brown the shank all over. Remove the shank. Add the vegetables to the pan and roast them for five minutes over medium heat. Squeeze the oranges; grate the rinds of three. Add the juice and the grated rinds to the pan. Stir in the maple syrup, the white wine, the veal jus and the vegetable broth. Reduce the glaze by one-half, stirring frequently. Put the shank back in the pan and baste well. Braise slowly in the oven for 1 1/2 hours, basting liberally with the glaze every 10 minutes.

Ducks On The Roof Restaurant

Gracious dining for dinner only with continental service, comfortable surroundings amidst coveys of duck decoys, and breads baked on the premises.

Innkeepers:	Brian Lucop and John Tersigni
Address:	1430 Front Rd. South, Amherstburg, Ont. N9V 3K1
Telephone:	519-736-6555
Rooms:	No accommodation
Children:	Yes
Open:	Year round. Closed Mondays. Dinner 5-8:30, Sun. 2-6:30
Food rates:	Dinner $$
Smoking:	No restrictions
Dress code:	Come as you are
Wheelchairs:	Dining room accessible; washrooms not accessible
Directions:	On Highway 18, 3 km (2 miles) south of Amherstburg, about 27 km (17 miles) south of Windsor

Yes, there are ducks on the roof of this fine restaurant. The first batch was put there back in the 1950s, when the place was known as Bell's Triangle Lodge and was operated as a hunting and fishing camp.

Sportsmen rented rooms above the present-day dining room or cabins on the shores of the nearby Detroit River, just upstream from where it enters Lake Erie. The name Bell's Triangle Lodge rapidly gave way to Ducks on the Roof, and when Brian and John bought the business as a restaurant in 1987, they kept the name . . . and the ducks.

The place already had a three-decade-strong reputation for fine food; they improved on it and added European-style service.

At last count there were 117 duck replicas scattered through the 75-seat restaurant, which has comfortable pine chairs and tables and a casual country ambience. Although the service in the restaurant is formal, there is no formal dress code. The owners say the bulk of their regular patrons are from nearby Detroit and its suburbs and 60 per cent of them dress casually; 40 per cent of the gentlemen wear neckties.

All principal dishes are accompanied by bread baked daily on the premises, soup of the day, a pear-shaped potato croquette and attractively arranged vegetables served in an individual steamer basket. The soup is served from pewter pots at tableside; salads are made at the table and some dishes are served at the table direct from the cooking dish. A number of entrees are also flamed at tableside.

One of the house specialties — as might be expected — is half a roasted duck with choice of apricot or honey garlic sauce, flamed at the table. There's also the full range of steaks, lamb, fish, quail, rabbit, chicken and shellfish.

This recipe provides an idea of the sort of appetizers available.

Ducks on the Roof Pâté
(Serves 10–12)

3 cups chicken livers	4 oz port
1 medium onion, chopped	Pinch thyme
Sautéed dried bread crumbs	2 cloves garlic
2 eggs	1 t green peppercorns
1 oz brandy	About 12 slices uncooked bacon

Pass chicken livers and onion through a meat grinder. At the end of the operation add enough dried bread crumbs to clean out the grinder. Put the eggs, brandy, port, thyme, garlic and peppercorns in a blender and liquefy. Add to chicken livers and blend well. Spray a small loaf pan (9 by 3 by 2 1/2 inches) with non-stick coating and line with bacon slices. Pour pâté mixture into pan and cover with bacon. Bake at 400° F for about 75 minutes or until the liquid is bubbling clear.

Using a second, similar-sized pan, press firmly to remove as much of the liquid as possible. Cool to room temperature and refrigerate. Will keep, refrigerated, for about 10 days, or portions may be frozen.

The Ancaster Old Mill Inn

Fine dining at an historic mill that still produces flour for bread baked daily on the premises. Mill tours and a gift shop of Canadian-made items.

Innkeepers:	Ron and David Ciancone
Address:	548 Old Dundas Rd., Ancaster, Ont. L9G 3J4
Telephone:	416-648-1827
Rooms:	No accommodation
Children:	Yes
Open:	Year round. Lunch, Mon.-Sat. 11:30-2:30; Dinner, Mon.-Thurs. 4:30-9, Fri.-Sat. 4:30-11, Sun. 4-9; Sunday brunch 10-2
Food rates:	Lunch $; Dinner $$
Smoking:	No restrictions, no-smoking area
Dress code:	Appropriate to fine dining
Facilities:	Glass-walled dining rooms overlooking the four-story mill and waterfalls can accommodate up to 450 diners
Attractions:	A live dinner theatre offers theme, contemporary, historical or mystery performances. Visitors may take a tour of the working mill and visit a gift shop well stocked with Canadian-made gift items
Wheelchairs:	All dining rooms and the gift shop are accessible

Directions: From Highway 403 west of Hamilton, take Mohawk Road West exit to Wilson St. in Ancaster. Turn right to Montgomery Drive, turn left and follow signs.

The 1863 four-story stone mill you'll admire while having a memorable lunch or dinner at The Ancaster Old Mill is the fourth to have been built on the property since 1792; the first three burned. The site has seen a lot of Canadian history.

One incredible tale that had a happy ending is told on the Old Mill's menu. Understandably, the menu doesn't tell another historical story, that of the trial of 19 men for treason following the War of 1812. The men were held in the Ancaster mill until a specially convened court reached its verdict — one so grisly the trial became known as the Bloody Assizes. The court ordered 11 of the men banished to a penal colony in what is now Tasmania. The other eight were ordered hanged, drawn and quartered.

When the Ciancone brothers decided to open a restaurant on the site, they didn't mess around with the architectural integrity of the property. Diners enter the old mill, cross a bridge over the mill stream and are inside a modern building before they realize it.

Through the glass walls they can admire the historic mill, the waterfall and mill stream. The dining areas are bright and spacious with lots of hanging plants, and the fittings and fixtures make you believe you're in one of the old mill buildings.

The menu is extensive, inventive and enticing. You know as you place your order that you'll have to return to try another of the entrees and certainly another of the seductive desserts.

Bread served with meals at the Old Mill is made from flour ground on the original mill stones, and the chef has kindly permitted publication of one of his bread recipes. You can buy bags of flour ground on the Old Mill's original stones at the gift shop. But if you want to try the following recipe before visiting, substitute any whole wheat flour.

The Ancaster Old Mill 100% Stone Ground Whole Wheat Bread

(Makes 2 loaves)

1 t brown sugar
2 1/4 cups warm water
2 pkg dry yeast
6-7 cups stone ground flour

3/4 cup dry powdered milk
1/2 cup brown sugar
2 t salt
1/3 cup cooking oil

Dissolve 1 t brown sugar in warm water and add yeast. Let stand 10 minutes. In a large mixing bowl, combine 5 cups flour, powdered milk, 1/2 cup brown sugar and salt. Stir in yeast mixture and oil. Stir in enough of remaining flour to make soft dough. Knead until smooth. Let rise in a warm place until doubled (about one hour). Punch down, divide and form into two loaves. Place in well-greased 8 1/2-inch loaf pans. Let rise in a warm place 45–60 minutes. Bake 15 minutes at 400° F. Reduce temperature to 350° F and bake 30 minutes longer or until loaves are nicely browned.

The Albion Hotel

A lively country pub ambience with licensed patio, basic bed and breakfast rooms and well-presented basic food.

Innkeepers:	Kim Muszynski and Harry Young
Address:	P.O. Box 114, Main St., Bayfield, Ont. N0M 1G0
Telephone:	519-565-2641
Rooms:	7; 1 with bathroom en suite, other 6 rooms share 2 bathrooms
Children:	Yes
Pets:	Yes
Open:	Year round. May–Thanksgiving, Mon.–Sat. 11:30–midnight; Sun. noon–11. Thanksgiving–April, Thurs.–Sun. 11:30–midnight, closed Mon., Tues., Wed.
Room rates:	$$, including continental breakfast. Off-season packages available
Food rates:	Lunch $; Dinner $$; Pub grub $
Smoking:	No restrictions
Dress code:	No shoes, no shirt, no service
Facilities:	Dining room; dining area in pub
Attractions:	Near public beach and marina on Lake Huron; boutiques; near Huron Country Playhouse; Blyth Festival; Goderich Township Windmill; next door to Ontario's best french-fried potatoes at the Admiral Bayfield
Wheelchairs:	Patio, bar, dining room accessible; washrooms and guest rooms not accessible
Directions:	On the main street of Bayfield near Clan Gregor Square

The enthusiasm of its young owners and staff make this 1840s yellow-brick landmark on the village's main street the "in" place of the fun crowd year round.

Bayfield, a village of 900 on a bluff overlooking Lake Huron, is one of only a handful of scenic spots in southwestern Ontario. It has a good sandy beach, a modern marina and Clan Gregor Square, a park-like square at its entrance from Highway 21 that is the scene of picnics and family reunions through the summer.

But for the clutter of automobiles in summer, Bayfield's main street has a nineteenth-century mood; the sidewalks are shaded by venerable willows and invite strolling, ice-cream cone in hand. Relics of the past are sold from half a dozen antique shops and boutiques.

The inn's guest rooms are all on the second floor and overlook either the main street or the gardens of neighboring homes. The size and furnishings of each room are different, and most of the furniture is from the original hotel, which started in 1857.

The 26-seat dining room keeps busy through the day, yet the dining area of the pub side of the first floor appears to draw even better. The room is dominated by the magnificent original wooden bar with brass foot rail.

The Albion's dinner menu runs to locally caught Lake Huron pickerel and perch, baby back ribs, chicken wings, the popular Albion burger and shrimp dishes, with a couple of steak options and a daily pasta special. All desserts are made in-house.

Here's the recipe for one of the Albion's more popular menu items.

The Albion Seafood Lasagna

(Serves 6)

1/2 cup butter	1/4 t nutmeg
1 onion, chopped	2 cups 18% cream
3/4 lb mushrooms, sliced	2 cups chicken stock
1/2 cup dry white wine	1 lb shelled, cooked shrimp
1/2 t parsley	1/4 lb combined crab meat and scallops
1/3 cup all purpose flour	9 lasagna noodles
3/4 t salt	3/4 lb sliced Swiss cheese
1/4 t ground pepper	1/4 cup grated Parmesan cheese

In a large saucepan over medium heat, melt 1/4 cup butter. Add onion and cook until soft. Add mushrooms and sauté for five minutes. Pour wine over mushrooms and onions, sprinkle with parsley and let simmer in saucepan, uncovered, until reduced by half. In another saucepan, melt remaining 1/4 cup butter, add flour and cook, stirring, for one minute. Season with salt, pepper and nutmeg. Slowly pour in cream and chicken stock, stirring constantly until thickened. Simmer two minutes. Add the mushroom-wine mixture and combine. Remove from heat.

In a large pot of boiling water, cook lasagna noodles for 10–12 minutes or until tender but firm. Drain and rinse under cold water; drain well.

In a bowl, mix the shrimp, crab meat and scallops. In a greased 9- by 13-inch baking dish, pour in one-third of the sauce, cover with one-third of the noodles, cover with one-third of the seafood and cover that with one-third of the Swiss cheese. Repeat until you have three layers each of sauce, seafood and cheese, ending with the Swiss cheese as the last layer. Sprinkle the top with grated Parmesan cheese. Bake, uncovered, at 350° F for 40 to 50 minutes or until bubbly and hot.

The Little Inn of Bayfield

Ontario's oldest continuously operated inn (since 1832) has been faithfully restored, and today's guest can enjoy a suite with fireplace and whirlpool.

Innkeepers:	Patrick and Gayle Waters
Address:	P.O. Box 100, Main St., Bayfield, Ont. N0M 1G0
Telephone:	519-565-2611
Rooms:	31 rooms and suites all with bathroom en suite
Children:	Yes
Pets:	No
Open:	Year round, daily 8 a.m.–9:30 p.m. Lunch 12–3; Afternoon tea 3–5; Dinner 5:30–9:30; Sunday brunch 11:30–2:30
Room rates:	$$$$. Seniors' rates. Off-season packages available
Food rates:	Lunch $; Dinner $$
Smoking:	In designated areas only
Dress code:	Country casual
Facilities:	Two dining rooms; licensed patio in manicured, shaded grounds; whirlpool, sauna, fireplaces and whirlpools in some rooms
Attractions:	Near public beach and marina on Lake Huron; boutiques; near Huron Country Playhouse; Blyth Festival; Goderich Township Windmill
Wheelchairs:	All public rooms and some guest rooms accessible
Directions:	On the main street of Bayfield

When the film industry gets around to an epic production on the early days of Ontario, the long shot of a stage coach pulling up in front of Bayfield's Little Inn won't require a lot of preparation. Nor will the local street scenes of horses and buggies and ladies with parasols and hoop skirts. They'll just have to cover the asphalt, lay down a plank sidewalk and hide the modern streetlights. Bayfield is that kind of place, and its premier inn belongs on such a movie set.

Nor has the march of what marketers call "progress" had a nasty impact on the inside of The Little Inn. The wood floors, oversize sideboards, wide hallways and handsome woodwork is all in place along with many examples of fine antique furniture. The mood created is one that invites a good read by the fire in the lounge by the small bar — and perhaps a doze — in a huge, well-broken-in easy chair.

The inn's best traditions have been preserved as well. Morning coffee is an occasion, and so is afternoon tea. Baking from the kitchen is served at both, and Devon cream and preserves accompany the scones at tea.

During 1984, the Waters expanded The Little Inn's accommodation facilities by adding 10 units in the former carriage house, now connected to the inn by a second dining room. The cottage suites with fireplaces and whirlpools are in the Guest Cottage, a separate building built in 1987, and the indoor pool, sauna and whirlpool are in the addition. The changes were made with the blessing of the Ontario Heritage Board, and the results should satisfy the most nit-picking history buff. The size and layout of each room is different, but all have antique furnishings and quiet color schemes.

The inn's cuisine runs to the freshest of produce, using local vegetables and fruit in season and Lake Huron fish landed at the harbor. The baking is all done in-house, and some of the preserves, sauces and dressings are bottled here and sold in the gift shop.

Chef/manager Richard Fituossi has kindly provided the recipe for one of the inn's popular treatments of Lake Huron fish.

The Little Inn Paupiettes of Pickerel with Shallot and Cream Saffron Sauce

(Serves 2)

1 t salt	1 egg
3 pickerel fillets, skin on	2 T white wine
9 fresh shrimp, peeled and deveined	1/2 t Pernod
3 slices bacon	Saffron sachet
1 ice cube	1/4 cup 35% cream
1 T cornstarch	Pepper to taste
Pinch cayenne	1 T butter
Pinch ground cloves	4 small new potatoes, steamed
1 shallot	22 snow peas, lightly stir fried in butter

Sprinkle 1/2 t salt over 2 pickerel fillets. Refrigerate. Skin remaining fillet. In food processor, place skinned fillet, 3 shrimp, bacon, 1/2 t salt, ice cube, cornstarch, cayenne, cloves, shallot and egg. Purée until smooth. Roll up salted fillets, skin side out, and hold them with toothpicks. Using a piping bag, stuff the center of the rolled fillets with the fish mixture. Force three shrimp into the middle of each, leaving the tails hanging over the sides of the roll. Place rolled fillets in a small baking dish filled with 1 cup of water, and cover tightly. Bake at 400° F for 20 minutes or until internal temperature is 150° F. Remove fillets from baking dish, preserving cooking liquids. Keep fillets warm.

To make the sauce: Over high heat, bring cooking liquid in the baking dish to a high boil and reduce by half. Add white wine, Pernod, saffron, cream, pepper and butter. Reduce, stirring frequently, until smooth and silky.

To serve: Make a clock face on each plate. Place two steamed potatoes at 12 o'clock and 11 snow peas at the remaining hours. Place one paupiette in the center of each plate and pour the sauce over. Serve very hot.

Beachburg Inn

A turn-of-the-century home converted to an English country inn lookalike with two guest rooms and offering traditional English dishes in three small dining areas.

Innkeepers:	David Miles and Ken Fink
Address:	161 Main St., Beachburg, Ont. K0J 1C0
Telephone:	613-582-3585
Rooms:	2 rooms, sharing bathroom and private sitting room
Children:	In dining rooms; not in guest rooms
Pets:	No
Open:	April–Oct. Closed Tuesdays. Lunch 11:30–2; Dinner 6–9; Sunday brunch 11–1:30. Dinners by reservation only
Room rates:	$, including full breakfast
Food rates:	Lunch $; Dinner $$
Smoking:	No restrictions
Dress code:	Come as you are
Facilities:	Two small dining rooms each seating 20 guests and a glass-enclosed verandah for 12
Attractions:	Near facilities for rafting the Ottawa River; swallow roost at Pembroke; Logos Land theme park and Storyland
Wheelchairs:	Not accessible
Directions:	In downtown Beachburg, off Highway 14 at County Road 21

Beachburg is a quiet village of 684 people on the Ottawa River about midway between Pembroke and Renfrew. The area is Ontario's whitewater-rafting capital, and a number of outfitters offer a variety of packages.

Beachburg Inn is a lovely, solid-looking building, formerly a private residence. The guest rooms are cozy and comfortably furnished with antiques. Two dining rooms and a glass-enclosed verandah are tastefully decorated with eye-catching antiques. If something really catches your fancy you can take it home with you — after paying for it — since most of the decorations in the inn are for sale.

The inn's lunch menu reads like one you'd find in a small English country inn. There are home-style soups and salads, dishes like shepherd's pie, ploughman's lunch and steak and kidney pie. There's a daily soup and a quiche of the day. The Cornish pasties and breads are all baked on the premises.

The inn's dinner specialty is roast lamb. There are chicken dishes and fish plates, and the selection of desserts, all made in-house, challenge the strong-willed dieter. David and Ken have shared the recipe for one of those desserts.

Beachburg Inn Sinful Chocolate Pie

Crust
3/4 cup icing sugar
1/3 cup cocoa
1/4 t salt
1/3 cup butter
1 cup finely chopped walnuts

Filling
1 pkg unflavored gelatin
2 T instant coffee granules
1/4 cup hot water
1 cup granulated sugar
1/2 cup cocoa
2 cups whipping cream
1 T coffee liqueur or 1 t vanilla extract

To make the crust: Blend the icing sugar, cocoa and salt. Melt butter until bubbling and add to the cocoa mixture, mixing well. Add the chopped walnuts and stir well. Press the mixture into the bottom and sides of a 9-inch pie plate.

To make the filling: Sprinkle gelatin and instant coffee granules over the hot water. Stir until dissolved and let cool. In a bowl, combine the sugar, cocoa, cream and liqueur (or vanilla); whip. Gently fold in the gelatin mixture. Pour the filling into the pie crust and chill at least 2 hours.

Angeline's Restaurant (Bloomfield Inn)

Fine French cuisine with continental service in an 1864 Victorian farm home and an adjoining spotlessly clean and recently renovated nine-unit motel-style inn.

Innkeeper:	Wilhelm Fida
Address:	29 Stanley St. West, Bloomfield, Ont. K0K 1G0
Telephone:	613-393-3301
Rooms:	9 modern motel units all with bathroom en suite
Children:	Yes
Pets:	Yes
Open:	Year round, closed six weeks in Jan. and Feb. Closed Tuesdays and Wednesdays except in July and Aug. Lunch noon–2; Dinner 5:30–9; Afternoon tea in July and Aug. 2–4:30. Reservations essential for dinner
Room rates:	$$. Off-season packages available
Food rates:	Lunch $; Dinner $$$
Smoking:	Smoke-free areas available
Dress code:	Casual
Facilities:	Three small dining rooms furnished with antiques and old oil paintings; outdoor patio; fully licensed
Attractions:	Near Lake on the Mountain; Sandbanks and North Beach provincial parks; Mariner's Museum Lighthouse Park; The Exotarium; Ameliasburgh Historical Museum

Wheelchairs: Dining rooms not accessible; one inn unit accessible
Directions: On the Loyalist Parkway near Picton, 29 km (18 miles) south of Belleville at the junction of County Roads 62 and 33

The Bloomfield Inn has a comfortable feel to it. It isn't one of those pretentious old mansions where the guest sometimes feels conversations ought to be whispered, in awe of the grand fixtures and fittings. Henry and Angeline Hubbs had the place built in 1869 as their home. And the new owners haven't messed around with the original floor plan or original woodwork.

Bloomfield is a quiet hamlet of under 700, at one time center for the local Quaker community, whose legacy remains in the two Quaker cemeteries and some fine old houses, well set back from the highway.

Angeline's lunch menu offers hors d'oeuvres, salads, soups, a daily special and only three entrees — steak, chicken and perch; there are Vienna-style desserts. The dinner menu has such treats as local pheasant breast with glazed raisins, fresh poached Atlantic salmon in a lemon cream sauce and golden caviar, and three variations of local lamb. There's also a low-calorie menu, or the exact opposite — a six-course "menu romantique Angeline."

The adjacent inn units have all been completely renovated. The new furniture is white maple. Four units have two double beds and five have one double bed. There's cable TV and air conditioning.

Wilhelm has shared the recipe for one of the popular desserts — for the serving of which he might be suspected of receiving kickbacks from the local Weight Watchers' treasurer.

Angeline's Raspberry Chocolate Cheesecake

Cheesecake layer

1 pkg (8 oz) cream cheese
1 cup icing sugar
1 egg yolk
1/2 t lime zest
3 T fresh lime juice
1 1/2 t unflavored gelatin
2 T water
1 cup whipping cream
1 9-inch sponge layer cake
1/3 cup raspberry jam
1/2 cup fresh raspberries

Mousse layer

1/2 lb bittersweet or semisweet chocolate
1 cup whipping cream
2 T granulated sugar
1 egg yolk
1 t rum

To make cheesecake layer: In a large bowl, beat cream cheese and icing sugar until fluffy. Beat in egg yolk, lime zest and lime juice. In small saucepan, stir gelatin into water and let soften a few minutes. Warm over low heat until melted and syrupy. Beat gradually into cream cheese mixture. Refrigerate until slightly firm but not set, about 20 minutes. Beat whipping cream; stir one-quarter into cream cheese mixture and fold in remainder. Line sides of a 9-inch springform pan with waxed paper. Place one cake layer, cut side up, in pan bottom. Spread with jam. Fold 1/2 cup of fresh raspberries into the cream cheese mixture. Spoon mixture over the cake, smoothing the top. Cover lightly and refrigerate.

To make mousse layer: Melt chocolate in double boiler over boiling water or in microwave oven at Medium. Meanwhile, in a deep bowl, whip cream with granulated sugar until firm. In a large bowl, beat egg yolk, gradually beating in chocolate. Working quickly, stir in about a quarter of the whipped cream and the rum. Fold in remaining cream.

To assemble: Spoon mousse over cheesecake layer, smoothing top. Cover and refrigerate until set, about 4 hours, or overnight. Cake can be covered and refrigerated up to 2 days. To serve, release sides of pan and gently pull off waxed paper. Transfer to doily-lined cake platter or stand. Use remaining berries as garnish or purée and strain them for a sauce to serve beside each wedge of cake.

The Maples Restaurant

*Fine dining with a European flair
in three rooms of an 1895 country home in a pretty
village on the Loyalist Parkway.*

Innkeepers:	Janey and Heinz Haas
Address:	148 Main St., P.O. Box 63, Bloomfield, Ont. K0K 1G0
Telephone:	613-393-3316
Rooms:	No accommodation
Children:	Yes
Open:	April–Thanksgiving, daily; Thanksgiving–Jan., Wed.—Sat. Closed Feb. and March. Lunch noon-2; Dinner 5-9
Food rates:	Lunch $; Dinner $$
Smoking:	In designated areas only
Dress code:	Country casual
Facilities:	Three dining rooms, fully licensed
Attractions:	Near Lake on the Mountain; Sandbanks and North Beach provincial parks; Mariner's Museum Lighthouse Park; The Exotarium; Ameliasburgh Historical Museum
Wheelchairs:	Accessible
Directions:	On the main street of the village of Bloomfield on the Loyalist Parkway (Highway 33)

Be certain of your facts should you wish to question something served to you at The Maples: your host teaches gourmet cooking to the hotel management students at Loyalist College in nearby Belleville.

But most nights you'll find Heinz whipping up wonders in his super-organized kitchen in the back of the lovely old frame village house that he and Janey have run as a restaurant since 1989. Heinz is the big guy in the white apron and the even whiter chef's hat. On a busy night he's a white blur with, it seems, a dozen sauces on the go and as many entrees in various stages of readiness.

Out front there's a main dining room and two smaller ones simply decorated with light paints and papers and framed paintings of local rural scenes. They are comfortable rooms; they're down-home and relaxing.

The lunch menu has four daily specials: soup, a sandwich, a croissant and a pasta dish. There are four salads, fish, liver, schnitzel, steak, egg dishes and chicken.

There's a wider choice in the evening: four treatments of chicken breast, three of steak and three schnitzels. One of the specialties is roasted loin of lamb with a herb and wine sauce. There are six fish dishes, including a daily special. All entrees are accompanied by vegetables and potato of the day.

Desserts feature local fruits in season and old favorites like pecan pie and carrot cake, and there's a selection of tortes. Rum Pot over ice cream is one of the favorites, and Heinz has been kind enough to share his technique for creating this delight.

The Maples Rum Pot

This is an investment of time and money and requires patience. You start the rum pot as fresh fruits begin coming in season and continue it to the end of the season. Around Christmastime your efforts are ready to start paying dividends. You can use any of the following fruits: strawberries, cherries, raspberries, blackberries, apricots, peaches, plums, grapes, currants, melons, pears, pineapple.

Use a crock pot or large Mason jar or any large glass bottle with a secure top. For every pound of fruit you need half a pound of fruit sugar. Peaches, pears, plums, apricots, melon and pineapple should be peeled and cut in small pieces. Clean berries gently. Put the fruit in the pot, add the sugar and add enough amber rum to cover the fruit in your container by two fingers. You can also use a mix of 2/3 amber rum, 1/3 brandy. As each fruit comes along, add another layer and top up with rum or the rum and brandy mix.

Never stir.

Keep the jar covered and in a cool place.

Three months after adding the last layer of fruit and topping up the rum, you can start enjoying your rum pot. Ladle the fruit and juice over ice cream, yogurt, a cheesecake, or — if you have a designated driver — have a bowlful on its own!

Inn at the Falls, 1862

A popular full-service country inn with fine food in pub and dining room. The patio, most rooms in the inn and all in the motel-type annex overlook a lovely waterfall.

Innkeepers:	Jan and Peter Rickard
Address:	17 Dominion St., P.O. Box 1139, Bracebridge, Ont. P0B 1C0
Telephone:	705-645-2245
Rooms:	18 rooms and suites all with bathroom en suite
Children:	Yes
Pets:	No
Open:	Year round. Mon.-Sat. 8 a.m.-midnight; Sun. 8 a.m.-11 p.m.
Room rates:	$$$$, Off-season packages available
Food rates:	Lunch $; Dinner $$; Pub food $
Smoking:	No restrictions
Dress code:	Jacket preferred in dining room
Facilities:	Outdoor heated swimming pool; outdoor shuffleboard; fireplaces in some rooms
Attractions:	Cruises on Lake Muskoka; Santa's Village; near Bethune Memorial House; Muskoka festival; cruises on R.M.S. *Segwun*
Wheelchairs:	Patio, pub and most guest rooms accessible

Directions: Take the Bracebridge exit from Highway 11 north, cross the bridge over the Muskoka River and turn left on Ontario St. Turn left on Dominion St. The inn is on your left at the bottom of the hill.

The turret-topped former private mansion was built in 1863 on the best site from which to appreciate the beauty of Bracebridge Falls on the Muskoka River.

It became an inn in 1943 and had a succession of owners until Jan and Peter bought the property in 1988. They decided they wanted to offer the upscale market a very special getaway retreat as well as provide the community and passersby in the know with a classy country pub and a venue for those special lunches or dinners. They brought to Bracebridge hospitality-industry expertise amassed during their 27-year apprenticeship at posh hotels and resorts from Bermuda to the Far East.

There are five guest rooms and two suites in the original mansion, all furnished with antiques. The bedroom suite in one room was owned in the 1880s by the governor-general of Bermuda. A sleigh bed in another room once belonged to Sir William Mulock, appointed Canada's postmaster general in 1896 by Sir Wilfrid Laurier.

Three pianos are scattered through the building, around which guests are welcome to sing — particularly in the pub, one of the few credible English-style pubs in the province. Rooms in the Mews, a two-story motel-type annex, command the best view of the falls through large picture windows. All have been completely redone with light and bright colors. Each has two double beds or a queen-size bed, and six have gas-burning fireplaces.

Jan and Peter boast that their inn serves "the best steak and kidney pie this side of the Atlantic" and were kind enough to share the recipe.

Inn at the Falls Steak and Kidney Pie

(Serves 20)

5 lbs New York striploin, diced
3 lbs beef kidneys, diced
2 bay leaves
1 T pepper
1 T chef's seasoning
30 oz plum tomatoes, diced
1 Spanish onion, diced

4 lbs mushrooms
19 oz tomato juice
8 oz red wine
1/2 cup all purpose flour
1/2 cup HP sauce
8 oz water
1 pkg frozen puff pastry, thawed

Boil diced steak and kidneys with bay leaves, pepper and chef's seasoning in enough water to cover. After 15 minutes, strain. Rinse with cool tap water and let drain. Mix meat with tomatoes, onions, mushrooms, tomato juice, wine, flour and HP sauce; add 8 oz water. Bake in a casserole at 400° F 30 minutes. Spoon into 20 oven-proof serving bowls. Cut and mold puff pastry sheet over each bowl. Brush pastry with egg wash and bake for 15 minutes or until pastry is puffed and golden.

Portions can be frozen in their individual bowls.

Café 13

A bistro-style restaurant and adjoining bar, both decorated with antiques in a gray granite building constructed in 1862 for the Imperial Bank of Canada.

Innkeepers:	Audrey and Blair Bender
Address:	13 Main St. West, Cambridge, Ont. N1R 5W1
Telephone:	519-621-1313
Rooms:	No accommodation
Children:	Special children's menu
Open:	Year round. Lunch, Mon.–Sat. 11–1; Dinner, Mon.–Thurs. until 11, Fri. and Sat. until midnight. Late-night snack menu after 9 daily. Closed Sundays and statutory holidays
Food rates:	Lunch $; Dinner $$
Smoking:	No pipes or cigars in dining room
Dress code:	Casual
Facilities:	Dining room furnished with antiques; turn-of-the-century American-style bar; extensive wine list.
Attractions:	Close to Doon Heritage Crossroads; Woodside National Historic Park; Kitchener Farmers' Market; Colonel John McCrae homestead in Guelph; Seagram Museum; Stratford Festival

Wheelchairs: Dining room and bar accessible; washrooms not accessible
Directions: In downtown Cambridge (formerly Galt) at corner of Main and Water St. (Hwy. 24), known locally as "four banks corner"

Before it got swallowed with Hespeler and Preston into a sprawling city with three downtown sections, Galt was known as the Granite City. Café 13 is in the heart of that attractive and historic area, occupying part of what's still known as the Granite Block.

On a cold, drizzly day in the heart of old Galt you could for an instant believe you'd wound up in Glasgow or Edinburgh; there are severe gray stone buildings in all directions. In better weather, enjoy this very pretty downtown section with its architectural gems and delicate church steeples along the banks of the Grand River, which used to power numerous grist and lumber mills in the town.

The enduring architecture is the legacy of disastrous fires in 1850 and 1860, after the last of which the downtown merchants decreed that all new buildings on Main St. would be made of stone.

Café 13 is a comfortable, informal place with Art Deco pieces and miscellaneous artifacts on the walls above tables and booths. Service is fast and professional, and you'll hear a lot of first names exchanged, particularly at lunch, which has a regular following of young professionals from the downtown area.

The menu is one of those glossy cardboard statements that keeps folding out to reveal more interesting offerings. Despite some horrendous puns, it's a bonanza for the à la carte sampler. If you brought a large appetite, there are full-course meals with steaks up to 16 ounces, back ribs, chicken, salmon, seafood and other plates with all the trimmings.

Trois Filet Teriyaki is one of the restaurant's very popular dishes, and manager Stephen Watson has made the recipe available.

Café 13 Trois Filet Teriyaki

(Serves 2)

3 oz pork tenderloin
3 oz boneless chicken breast

3 oz beef tenderloin

Teriyaki sauce

1 clove garlic, finely chopped
1 small onion, finely chopped
1/4 cup soy sauce
2 1/2 oz dry white wine
1 T tomato paste
2 oz gravy or brown sauce

2 T brown sugar
1/2 oz Realemon
2 oz pineapple juice
1 T cornstarch
1/4 cup sliced water chestnuts
Sliced green onions and sesame seeds for garnish

Sauté garlic and onion in butter until brown. Add soy sauce, 2 oz wine, tomato paste, gravy or brown sauce, brown sugar, Realemon and pineapple juice; cook until reduced by half. Strain. Thicken with cornstarch blended with a little water.

Trois filet: Cut meat into strips. Pan fry the pork and chicken thoroughly. Pan fry the beef to desired degree. Drain excess fat. Deglaze pan with 1/2 oz white wine. Add sliced water chestnuts and teriyaki sauce to pan and cook 1 minute.

To serve, arrange meats on platter, cover with sauce and garnish with sliced green onions and sesame seeds.

Langdon Hall Country House Hotel

A magnificent Colonial Revival mansion in 40 landscaped acres sensitively adapted to a full-service grand country hotel.

Innkeepers:	William Bennett and Mary Beaton
Address:	R.R. 33, Cambridge, Ont. N3H 4R8
Telephone:	519-740-2100
Rooms:	39 rooms, 2 suites, all with bathroom en suite
Children:	Yes
Pets:	Not in rooms; kennels are provided on grounds
Open:	Year round, daily. Lunch, Mon.–Fri. noon–2, Sat.–Sun. until 2:45, Dinner 6:30–9:30; Afternoon tea, May–Sept., daily 3–6, Oct.–Apr., Fri.–Sun. only.
Room rates:	$$$$$$. Weekend and midweek packages available
Food rates:	Lunch $$; Dinner $$$$$; Bar dinner $$$
Smoking:	No smoking in dining room
Dress code:	Jacket preferred in dining room
Facilities:	6 meeting rooms; conservatory and drawing rooms with fireplaces; outdoor heated swimming pool; sauna and whirlpool; exercise equipment; billiard room; card room; canoeing on the Grand River; ballooning; tennis; croquet; hiking trails; 30 of the rooms have wood-burning fireplaces; 24-hour room service

Attractions: Close to Doon Heritage Crossroads; Woodside National Historic Park; Kitchener Farmers' Market; Colonel John McCrae homestead in Guelph; Seagram Museum; Stratford Festival
Wheelchairs: All public rooms and most guest rooms accessible
Directions: Take Exit 275 (Homer Watson Blvd.) from Highway 401. Exit 275 is west of Highway 8 to Kitchener/Waterloo. Travel south on Fountain Street/Homer Watson Blvd., to Blair Road, the second road on your right, and follow the signposts to Blair. Go through Blair, past the town tavern to Langdon Road, the second on your right. Turn at the first driveway on the left and follow the lane into Langdon Hall.

The driveway winds through a stand of ancient pines, and just when you start thinking you've taken a wrong turning, the road swings out of the woods to the bottom of acres of lawn sloping up to the hall.

The 1898 summer mansion built for a great-grandson of John Jacob Astor is as striking today as it was then; perhaps even more so because such homes are no longer built, and fire and the wrecker's ball are shrinking this country's modest inventory of them.

William Bennett and Mary Beaton carefully protected the integrity of Langdon Hall's mood. Although the home has been converted to a country hotel, the visitor still feels like the personal guest of the owner.

The reception desk just inside the grand front door doesn't seem like a reception desk. It seems like a station for one of the servants to point guests to their room, the conservatory or the lounge or dining rooms.

Open fireplaces in the vast rooms crackle on chilly days, and hallways and public rooms are decorated with a fabulous collection of period paintings, nineteenth-century porcelain pieces and antique furniture.

There are 13 guest rooms on the second and third floors of the hall, each of a different configuration and size. Their washrooms all have pedestal-style wash basins and cast-iron bathtubs encased in mahogany. Half a dozen of the hall's guest rooms have wood-burning fireplaces, some have sleeping lofts and most have handsome pieces of antique furniture.

The other 28 rooms are in an annex called The Cloisters, which is reached by underground passageway. The Cloisters is to one side of the hall overlooking the croquet lawn, swimming pool and change houses and doesn't compete with the hall's striking architecture. All rooms in The Cloisters have wood-burning fireplaces and contemporary furniture.

Rooms in the hall and annex have all the touches: terrycloth robes, hair dryers, bath gels, special soaps and shampoos.

Chef Nigel Didcock is English, though he trained in a number of prestigious kitchens in France, and his menus offer variations on dishes from both countries. Here's one of his creations.

Langdon Hall Goat Cheese Mousseline with Eggplant Confit

(Serves 4)

2 Italian eggplants	Selection of fresh herbs
3-4 oz goat cheese	Freshly ground black pepper
1 T 35% cream	

Marinade

1 small onion, sliced	2 T balsamic vinegar
1 tomato, seeded and sliced	1 t honey
2 cloves garlic	1/4 t white pepper
1 cup olive oil	Rock salt
4 T red wine vinegar	Thyme, rosemary, bay leaves
2 T sherry vinegar	

Slice the eggplants into rounds 1/8 inch thick. Combine all the marinade ingredients in a saucepan and simmer gently over low heat for 10 minutes. Add the sliced eggplant. Shake the pan so all slices of eggplant are submerged. Simmer for a further 10 minutes, remove from heat and marinate, covered, at room temperature for 48 hours.

When the eggplant has marinated for two days, place the goat cheese in a bowl, and stir in the cream, finely chopped herbs and a twist of pepper. Keep at room temperature until served.

To serve, fish eggplant slices out of the marinade. Arrange four slices in the center of a plate, slightly overlapping. With two dessert spoons heated in hot water, form a quenelle (olive-shaped ball) of cheese mixture and place it on the eggplant. Use the marinade as a dressing and garnish with fresh herbs. The eggplant may be served hot, if desired.

The Opinicon

A family owned and operated full-service summer resort with rooms in the hotel, cottages in the woods and a fine dining room for guests and those with reservations.

Innkeepers:	Al and Janice Cross
Address;	Chaffey's Locks, R.R. 1, Elgin, Ont. K0G 1C0
Telephone:	613-359-5233
Rooms:	18 rooms in the hotel, all with bathroom en suite; 19 cottages of different sizes, some with fireplace. Cottages can accommodate from 2 to 8 persons
Children:	Yes
Pets:	Yes
Open:	Mid-April to mid-Nov. Breakfast 7:30-9; Lunch noon-1:30; Dinner 6-8
Room rates:	$$$$$$, including three meals per day. Weekly rates; discounts in spring and fall
Food rates:	Lunch $; Dinner $$. Non-guests must make reservations
Note:	No credit card, but personal cheques accepted
Smoking:	In designated areas
Dress code:	Casual
Facilities:	The dining room is not licensed. A coffee bar is open throughout the day for light meals and a store offers snacks, mixes and sundries. Heated swimming pool, shuffleboard, children's playground, croquet, lending library, horseshoe pitch, tennis courts, ping pong, volleyball, badminton, fishing, boating, on 17 acres with mature trees and flower gardens

Attractions:	All water sports; boating on the Rideau Canal, which abuts the property; antique shops; hiking; rockhounding; historic sites; small Lockmaster's House Museum across the road
Wheelchairs:	Dining room, meeting rooms, 5 guest rooms on the first floor of the hotel and some cabins accessible
Directions:	From eastbound Highway 401, take Exit 623 (past Kingston), turn north on Highway 15, follow to 3 km (2 miles) past Elgin, turn left on Chaffey's Locks Road (Country Road 9).

Today there's a wider choice of cuisine, electric lights and no problems when you want a hot shower or bath. But not a lot else has changed from the 1860s, when this magnificent mansion was home of the Chaffey family and their guests.

The tradition of gracious hospitality has been carried on since the Jarrett family converted the estate into a resort in 1921. Their updating and modernizing over the years has not intruded on the grandeur of the original home or its beautiful wooded site at Chaffey's Locks on the Rideau Canal and Lake Opinicon.

Most of the rooms in the main hotel open on the deep porch or second-floor balcony and all are carpeted and have private bathrooms. The cottages are in a grove set back from the shoreline. All have one or two bathrooms, TV, electric heat, smoke detectors, refrigerators, and are carpeted. The larger units have living rooms with fireplaces and the smaller ones have screened porches.

All the usual resort sports and games are provided, and 20 lakes with bass and pike are easily accessible by boat from the resort through the Rideau Canal and lake system. Guides or boats are available for fishing or lake trips. The cottages are well separated from one another on the spacious property, and there are all sorts of places hotel guests can get away to by themselves with a book or to snooze in the sun.

The rates include three meals a day. The lunch and dinner menus have a wider choice than many restaurants. The lunch menu offers five appetizers, nine entrees and nine desserts. There are eight dinner entrees — dishes like roast prime rib of beef, roast Cornish game hen or roast leg of lamb — as well as fish, shrimp, veal and other lighter dishes. With advance notice, the hotel will provide box lunches for guests going fishing, taking cruises or just wandering off on a picnic or backroads drive.

Non-guests wishing to sample the cuisine in the airy dining room overlooking Lake Opinicon are welcome but must make reservations. The following recipe is the sort of mouth-watering dessert you're likely to find on the menu.

Opinicon Brown Sugar and Rhubarb Pie

9" unbaked pie shell
1 - 1 1/4 cups packed brown sugar
1/4 cup all purpose flour
1/4 t salt

4 cups diced rhubarb (about 1 pound)
3 eggs, separated
1 T lemon juice

Bake pastry in a 450° F oven for 5 minutes. Cool.

Combine brown sugar, flour and salt. Add sugar mixture to rhubarb; toss to coat well. Let stand 15 minutes. Beat egg yolks slightly with fork. Stir yolks and lemon juice into rhubarb. Turn rhubarb filling into partially baked pastry shell. Reduce oven temperature to 375° F and bake for 40–45 minutes, until nearly set. Pie will appear soft in center but becomes firm after cooling.

Meanwhile, using any meringue recipe, prepare meringue with egg whites. Spread over hot rhubarb filling and seal to edge. Reduce oven temperature to 350° F and bake pie for 12–15 minutes more. Cool before serving.

You can omit the meringue and serve the pie with whipped cream or ice cream.

Woodlawn Terrace Inn

An outstanding full-service historic country inn with 14 guest rooms and continental cuisine served in opulent surroundings graced with beautiful antiques.

Innkeepers:	Gerda and Domenico Della-Casa
Address:	420 Division St., Cobourg, Ont. K9A 3R9
Telephone:	416-372-2235
Rooms:	13 rooms, 1 suite, all with bathroom en suite
Children:	Yes
Pets:	No
Open:	Year round, daily. Lunch, Mon.–Fri. 11:30–2; Dinner 5:30–9; Sunday brunch 11:30–2
Room rates:	$$$. Winter packages and corporate rates available
Food rates:	Lunch $; Dinner $$
Smoking:	No-smoking area in dining room
Dress code:	Informal
Facilities:	3 fully licensed dining rooms; bar-lounge; meeting rooms
Attractions:	Victoria Hall; Art Gallery of Northumberland; The Big Apple; Heritage Harbor; Barnum House Museum; close to Peterborough and world's highest lift lock; Summer Festival of Lights; Home of Marie Dressler Memorabilia Museum; charter fishing; cross-country skiing
Wheelchairs:	All public rooms and most guest rooms accessible
Directions:	Take Exit 474 (Highway 45) from Highway 401. Follow south onto Division Street.

Cobourg has an overflowing cornucopia of magnificent historic buildings dating from 1828. One of the region's showplaces is Victoria Hall in downtown, built between 1856 and 1860 when Cobourg expected to be made capital of Upper Canada. Sixty-five buildings are listed by the Local Architectural Conservation Advisory Committee, and of those, 28 are designated under the Ontario Heritage Act.

In almost any other Ontario community, Woodlawn Terrace Inn would also enjoy such a designation. It's a striking Regency-style mansion built in 1835 by one of the first United Empire Loyalists to move to the area. Ebenezer Perry had served in the War of 1812, moved to Cobourg in 1815 and became first chairman of the Board of Police Commissioners, forerunner to town council for governing the town.

The home Perry built has a sweeping second-floor gallery, contrasting window sizes on the first and second floors, a low hip roof and tall brick chimneys. Guest rooms are on the first and second floors and differ in size and layout. Some are furnished with antiques and period furniture.

In the spacious public rooms on the main floor, many original pieces remain. There are open wood-burning fireplaces, massive antique sideboards and large crystal chandeliers.

Two wings were added to the mansion in the 1850s, but only the south wing remains. The present owners haven't tampered with the building's integrity of design to transform it into a grand country inn. Today's guest, though perhaps awed by the opulence, nevertheless feels like a personal guest of the owner.

The continental cuisine has a few Italian touches, understandable when the chef is your host, Domenico Della-Casa. Two of the house specialties are veal saltimbocca alla Romano and beef tournedos aux morels, and on the appetizer list there are two pasta offerings.

The inn's dinner menu has specially prepared chicken and trout dishes for those watching their waistlines and two dishes that can be shared. The Entrecôte Amoureuse à la Dijonnaise and Chateaubriand bouquetière are both flambéed at your table. There are four seafood entrees, three steaks and 10 more entrees including veal, chicken, duckling, quail, lobster and lamb.

Woodlawn Terrace Inn's menu isn't just a pretty print job, and Della-Casa isn't a culinary dilettante: in 1990 his kitchen was presented the Silver Spoon Award by the Gourmet Diners Club of America.

Domenico offers the following recipe from his menu.

Woodlawn Terrace Fettuccini Victoria

(Serves 2)

1/4 lb fettuccini
1/4 cup butter
2 t chopped green onion (white part only)
1 1/2 cucumbers, cut in matchsticks
1 bunch dill, finely chopped

2 t horseradish
4 oz 18% cream
4 oz smoked salmon, cut in strips
Salt and black pepper to taste

In a pot of boiling water, cook fettuccini until tender but firm; drain and return to saucepan.

Meanwhile, in a frying pan, melt butter; add green onion and sauté until pale gold. Add cucumber, dill, horseradish and cream; simmer for a few minutes. Add drained pasta and salmon; simmer for a few minutes. Serve immediately.

The Spike and Spoon

Fine dining at reasonable prices, accented by home-grown herbs, served in a grand old mansion with loads of character and history.

Innkeepers:	Len and Frances Schaeffer
Address:	637 Hurontario St., Collingwood, Ont. L9Y 2N6
Telephone:	705-445-2048
Rooms:	No accommodation
Children:	Yes
Open:	Year round, except April and Nov. Lunch, Tues.–Fri. noon–2; Dinner, Tues.–Sat. 5:30–9. Closed Sundays and Christmas Eve and Christmas Day
Food rates:	Lunch $; Dinner $$; fixed-price menu (five courses) $$$$
Smoking:	No-smoking areas; no pipes or cigars in dining room
Dress code:	Casual
Facilities:	Three dining rooms, two with fireplaces
Attractions:	Blue Mountain Ski area; Blue Mountain Slide Rides; Scenic Caves; Collingwood Museum
Wheelchairs:	Dining rooms accessible
Directions:	On the main street of Collingwood; drive south (away from Georgian Bay) on Highway 24. The restaurant is on your left with parking in the rear.

Diners in this beautiful historic mansion of many parts find an interesting history lesson on the back of the menu, which explains the origin of the restaurant's unusual name. Here it is, in abbreviated form:

The spike, forerunner of the fork, was developed in England in the sixteenth century by those no longer content to wipe greasy fingers on their clothes. This utensil, similar to a long nail with a handle, was used by particularly fastidious people to push even their pudding onto their spoon, and brought upon them the title "spike and spoon people," which evolved to spick and span. The change to the spike caused opposition and one of the most interesting attacks was led by the Bishop of London. He preached a sermon on the evil of using forks . . . when we had been provided with fingers by God.

Equally interesting is the history of the restaurant building, which started as a humble farmhouse in the mid-1800s. It was extensively reworked in 1905 to coax an architect's son and daughter-in-law to leave their traveling circuses in Mexico and move closer to Dad. (The story is also told on a page of the dinner menu.)

Len and Frances opened their restaurant in 1972 after extensively renovating the mansion, and they've added a lot of personal touches. They make their own tablecloths, serve meals on Spode china, and grow their own herbs year round in a garden and winter solarium. From summer through fall vegetables come from the gardens at the rear of the property.

Menu offerings are limited but comprehensive and interestingly presented. The rack of lamb, for example, is served with herbed yogurt; grilled chicken breast is garnished with three-mustard butter and pan fried scallops are served under a lemon thyme cream sauce. There's a daily fish special depending on what's just been caught and is at the local market. Len and Frances have kindly made available this recipe for far-from-ordinary fare.

The Spike and Spoon Pear Mint Chutney

1 cup mint
2 onions
2 green peppers
6 pears
6 apples

1 1/2 cups raisins
4 cups white vinegar
5 cups white sugar
2 T salt
2 1/2 T mustard seed

Chop, grind or shred the mint, onions, peppers, pears, apples and raisins; set aside. Boil the vinegar, sugar, salt and mustard seed; pour over the fruit-vegetable mixture. Let stand, covered, at room temperature for one week, stirring every day. Bottle in sterilized jars and let stand for one month before using.

Hudson House

A beautifully wrought historic country inn in a bucolic setting on the banks of the Madawaska River.

Innkeepers:	Mechthild Thuemen and Ed Peplinskie
Address:	Mill St., Combermere, Ont. K0J 1L0
Telephone:	613-756-2326
Rooms:	No accommodation
Children:	Yes
Open:	April–Nov. daily, noon–10
Food rates:	Lunch $; Dinner $
Smoking:	In designated areas only
Dress code:	Country casual
Facilities:	2 licensed dining rooms; licensed patio on terrace overlooking Madawaska River
Attractions:	Near Bancroft Mineral Museum; Eagle's Nest Lookout; Bancroft Historical Museum; Bancroft Art Gallery; Madonna House Pioneer Museum at Combermere; deserted Craigmont Corrundum Mine near Combermere
Wheelchairs:	Accessible
Directions:	At the bridge on the Madawaska River and Highway 62, about 16 km (10 miles) south of Barry's Bay

When this lovely stone building overlooking the Madawaska River was restored and renovated in 1984, great care was taken to preserve the character built into it in 1912. That's when Capt. John Hudson rebuilt it for the second time after it was destroyed by fire. Captain Hudson wasn't able to enjoy his rebuilt home for long. He went down with his ship, the sternwheeler *Mayflower*, in November of that year. The night after the close of the regular sailing season was vicious, with heavy snow. But Captain Hudson had agreed to make one last trip between Barry's Bay and Combermere because his cargo was the body of a young man who had been killed in an accident in Saskatchewan and who was being brought home to Palmer Rapids for burial.

The Hudson House keeps alive the captain's name, and the building recalls an era of gracious living in less-hurried times. The spacious dining rooms overlook the river, and in fine weather diners can have pre- or post-prandial refreshments on a patio above terraced lawns that slope down to the river bank. A magnificent antique wooden bar dominates one of the dining rooms.

The list of offerings on the lunch and dinner menus is short but varied. The six appetizers are common to both menus: a soup of the day, two salads served with homemade dressings, French onion soup, cognac pâté and rollmops (pickled herring with sour cream).

At lunch there are seven sandwiches, farmer's sausage on a bun, a burger, corned beef on a kaiser and two pasta dishes. Frittata is an oven-baked combination of eggs, three cheeses, sautéed vegetables and herbs.

The dinner menu lists six entrees — a pasta dish, fish, scallops, Wiener schnitzel, baked ham and sirloin steak. Here's the recipe for one of their popular desserts.

Hudson House Chocolate Truffle Pie

Double chocolate chip cookies
4 T butter
1 pkg unflavored gelatin
1/3 cup cold orange juice
1 T instant coffee
6 oz semisweet chocolate chips

1 t vanilla extract
2 eggs
1/4 cup sugar
1 1/2 cups whipping cream
Melted chocolate for garnish

To make pie crust: In a food processor, grind up enough double chocolate chip cookies to make 1 1/2 cups of crumbs. Melt butter and mix with crumbs. Pat crumb mixture firmly into a 9-inch pie tin.

To make filling: In a medium saucepan, sprinkle gelatin over orange juice. Let stand 1 minute. Stir over low heat until gelatin dissolves. Add coffee and chocolate chips; heat, stirring constantly, until chocolate is melted. Remove from heat and stir in vanilla. Let stand 10 minutes.

Meanwhile in a large bowl with electric mixer at high speed, beat eggs with sugar until thickened. In a separate bowl, beat whipping cream until thick. Gradually add lukewarm gelatin mixture and beat lightly until just blended. Fold in whipped cream. Turn into prepared crust and chill until firm. To garnish, drizzle melted chocolate over firm pie.

The Riverview Lodge

A gem of a country inn with beautifully decorated large rooms and an inviting bar lounge, and offering some of the finest dining in all of northern Ontario.

Innkeepers:	Helen and Ross Durance; Suzanne and Barry Scherban; Susan Durance and Jordon Pailian
Address:	148 Earl Ave., Dryden, Ont. P8N 1Y1
Telephone:	807-223-4320
Rooms:	11 rooms, 1 suite, all with bathroom en suite
Children:	Yes
Pets:	No
Open:	Year round. Lunch, Mon.-Fri. 11:30-2; Dinner, Mon.-Sat. 5:30-9:30. Closed on major holidays
Room rates:	$$$, continental breakfast included; full breakfast available for room guests
Food rates:	Lunch $; Dinner $$
Smoking:	No restrictions
Dress code:	Casual
Facilities:	Jacuzzi bathtub, king-size beds, log decor in deluxe rooms; suite has original stone fireplace and roof deck patio; most guest rooms and public rooms overlook the Wabigoon River
Attractions:	Dryden & District Museum; Maximillian Moose; Egli's Sheep Farm; Canadian Pacific Forest Products tours
Wheelchairs:	Not accessible
Directions:	Two km (1 1/4 miles) south of Highway 17 and about a block south of Highway 594 (Duke St.) on a residential stretch of Earl Ave. Well signposted.

Don't let the unprepossessing appearance of the outside of Riverview Lodge let you falter for a second on your way to its warm, welcoming interior; the lodge is one of the real accommodation gems of the province.

A cozy bar gleams with brass and Tiffany stained glass. The elegant dining room is walled in tree trunks — the original walls of the log hotel built in 1912 for executives of the paper mill that is Dryden's raison d'être.

The rooms are exceptional. A "standard" room measures 15 by 30 feet, the deluxe rooms are even larger, and the suite is vast, and certainly more tastefully decorated than most suites in major hotels. In the deluxe rooms some of the walls are the original log walls, glistening under fresh varnish. Bathrooms are spacious and have large tubs.

The lunch menu offers good variety, but nothing you wouldn't find in any fine restaurant: salads, sandwiches made from croissants, soups, burgers, sandwiches with chicken filets, corned beef, prime rib and the ubiquitous steak sandwich.

But the dinner menu makes for difficult decisions, from inventive starters through tempting salads to about 20 entrees from lamb, beef and pork to shrimp, fish, veal and chicken. One interesting lodge specialty is Trois Viandes, a lamb chop and beef and pork medallions grilled and served with burgundy wine sauce. (Obviously inspired by dining with one of those types who can never make up his/her mind!)

Barry Scherban, executive chef of The Lodge (as it's known locally), has generously made available this recipe from the menu, a favorite of frequent guests.

Riverview Lodge Veal Medallions
(Serves 2)

8-10 oz veal loin or tenderloin
Salt and pepper to taste
Cooking oil or clarified butter
1 oz white wine
6 oz 35% cream
Fresh rosemary or paste

Slice veal into 8 medallions; flatten to uniform thickness, about 1/2 inch. Season with salt and pepper. Heat oil in heavy skillet. Add veal slices; sauté until centers are pink. Remove from pan and pour off excess oil. Deglaze pan with wine; reduce by half. Add cream and rosemary; simmer until slightly thickened. Arrange veal on plates and lightly spoon sauce over a portion of the medallions. Serve immediately.

Teddy Bear Bed and Breakfast Inn

A country inn chock-a-block with teddy bears and antiques with fine country-style dining for house guests or by reservation.

Innkeepers:	Gerrie and Vivian Smith
Address:	R.R. 1, Elmira, Ont. N3B 2Z1
Telephone:	519-669-2379
Rooms:	3 rooms
Children:	Yes
Pets:	No
Open:	Year round. Lunches during weekdays may be arranged for small private groups by reservation only. Dining room normally reserved for house guests only
Room rates:	$-$$, including full or deluxe breakfast
Food rates:	Lunch $$; Dinner $$$
Smoking:	No smoking
Dress code:	Semi-formal
Facilities:	Unlicensed dining room; large private guest lounge; TV; games room; seminar facility; library; lawn chairs
Attractions:	Near Elmira, Elora, Fergus, Kitchener-Waterloo in the heart of Mennonite country; windsurfing and sailing, hiking, ski trails

Wheelchairs: Not accessible
Directions: Just north of the village of Floradale. Floradale is 2 km (1 1/4 miles) west of Elmira and north on County Road 19/6.

There are teddy bears everywhere: the cuddly critters are propped against pillows atop Mennonite quilts on the guest-room beds; they smirk from vantage points on mantelpieces and bookcases, and even the hand soap is in the shape of a teddy bear and prints of them adorn the shower curtains and table napkins.

There are hundreds of them throughout the rambling, cozy home that Gerrie and Vivian have created from the 1907 Floradale school house, known as Wyndham Hall. The historic building atop a hill just outside the village of Floradale is essentially a bed and breakfast operation, but by arrangement guests may have all three meals served on white tablecloths in the dining room.

Downstairs there's a large lounge with wood-burning fireplace where guests may read or play board games or where people can gather for meetings or seminars. Throughout there are antiques and interesting knick-knacks, Mennonite quilts, wall hangings and rugs . . . and everywhere, teddy bears. Pets aren't welcome, but guests are invited to bring their teddy bears.

Wyndham Hall makes a comfortable, homey base from which to explore the picturesque and interesting villages of the region; to browse for Mennonite handcrafts, soak up the tranquil lifestyle or just stay put in the quiet country setting removed from the hassles of city living.

By arrangement, Vivian will provide all meals for guests in the large kitchen; much of the food is prepared over a wood stove. Following is the recipe for one of her more popular dishes.

Teddy Bear Beef Wyndham (Stroganoff)

(Serves 10)

4 lbs tenderloin tips
2 t salt
1/4 t pepper
1 cup all purpose flour
2/3 cup butter
1 cup finely chopped onions

3 10-oz cans consommé
1 lb mushrooms, sliced
6 T butter
2 cups sour cream
6 T tomato ketchup
2 t Worcestershire sauce

Slice tenderloin in strips about 2 by 1 by 1/4 inches. Mix salt and pepper with flour and dredge meat in flour mixture. In heavy pan over medium-high heat, heat 2/3 cup butter, add onions and meat, and brown meat on all sides. Stir in consommé. Cover and simmer 20 minutes. In a separate pan sauté mushrooms in 6 T butter. Blend together sour cream, tomato ketchup and Worcestershire sauce. Remove mushrooms from heat and add sour cream mixture in small amounts. *Do not boil or sour cream will separate.* Ladle meat, onion and consommé mixture over bed of noodles on each plate and top with mushroom and sour cream mixture.

The Elora Mill

Limestone walls and hand-hewn beams greet guests at one of Canada's few remaining five-story gristmills, converted to luxury accommodation and offering superb dining.

Innkeeper:	Timothy N. Taylor
Address:	77 Mill St. West, Box 218, Elora, Ont. N0B 1S0
Telephone:	519-846-5356
Rooms:	32, including 7 bedsitting and 4 suites, all with bathroom en suite
Children:	Yes
Pets:	No
Open:	Year round. Lunch, daily noon–2:30; Dinner, daily 5:30–9
Room rates:	$$$$, including continental breakfast
Food rates:	Lunch $; Dinner $$
Smoking:	No cigars or pipes in dining room
Dress code:	Country casual
Facilities:	Fully licensed lounge and dining room overlooking the cliff-lined gorge of the Grand River, flood-lighted at night
Attractions:	Hiking in the limestone canyon of the Elora Gorge; Elora Music Festival; near Fergus with its farmers' market, Fergus Highland Games, Great Teddy Bear Caper, Templin Gardens
Wheelchairs:	Dining room and some guest rooms accessible
Directions:	On the Grand River in the heart of Elora

In every room or hallway of The Elora Mill there's a section of original limestone wall or at the very least a hand-hewn wooden beam to remind the guest that this is a piece of Canadian history. The building was a working gristmill from 1859 until 1974, when it was bought by two Toronto entrepreneurs who then spent two years transforming the building into a beautiful full-service country inn.

There are 22 guest rooms in the mill building and 10 more rooms in three other historic stone buildings close by the mill. Some of the outlying rooms and suites have fireplaces.

The rooms have different configurations but all contain period pine furniture and quilts made by Mennonites in the area. The color scheme of each room starts with the hand-painted bathroom wash basins, and those vibrant or pastel colors are carried out into the room's decor. Framed prints of Elora in days gone by are in each room. The toilets have pull chains and some of the rooms have brass bedsteads.

The inn is in the heart of a village with historic stone buildings that could have been lifted from England's Cotswolds or southern France. The picturesque town swarms with tourists during warm weather, and the historic limestone architecture of the town lends itself to period films and TV commercials that seek to capture the mood of Europe or life in the early days of the North American colonies.

Elora has attracted numerous entrepreneurs who have opened gift shops, gourmet restaurants and boutiques in the historic stone buildings in the town's core along a quiet street which ends at the mill. The Scotsman who founded the village in 1832 named it in honor of his brother's ship, which in turn had been named after the cave temples of Ellora in India.

Chef Brian Holden has written menus that make comforting reading for lovers of fine food. The cuisine is a mix of Canadian and European dishes, and there are such imaginative entrees as Chicken Holden — chicken breast surrounding duck mousseline, spinach and mild Monterey Jack cheese, baked and served with a fresh cranberry and red currant sauce.

The inn's Caesar salad is a favorite of many guests, and Chef Brian has shared his recipe.

The Elora Mill World's Best Caesar

(Serves 2)

Freshly ground pepper
1 clove garlic
2 anchovy fillets
1 t Dijon mustard
2 egg yolks
1/4–1/2 cup olive oil (to taste)
Dash Tabasco
1 t Worcestershire sauce
1 t red wine vinegar
Juice of 1/2 lemon
1/2 head romaine, cleaned
1/2 cup grated Parmesan cheese
1/2 cup croutons

Crush ground pepper into salad bowl. Add garlic and anchovies and crush well. Add mustard to form a paste. Add egg yolks and mix. Slowly add oil while beating quickly with two forks; the texture of the dressing will thicken slightly. Add Tabasco, Worcestershire sauce, red wine vinegar and the lemon juice; mix well. Add lettuce and toss to coat. Add Parmesan cheese and croutons and toss again. Rub serving plates with remaining lemon half. Serve and top with freshly ground pepper.

The Emo Inn

A modern motel, lounge and dining room so well planned and tastefully decorated that it merits inclusion in this collection of mostly traditional country inns.

Innkeepers:	Ernie Sotke and Sharon Hagedorn
Address:	Highway 11/71, P.O. Box 598, Emo, Ont. P0W 1E0
Telephone:	807-482-2272
Rooms:	20 rooms all with bathroom en suite
Children:	Yes
Pets:	Yes
Open:	Year round. Dining room 7 a.m.–10 p.m.; Sunday brunch, 11–2
Room rates:	$$. Off-season packages available
Food rates:	Lunch $; Dinner $$; Pub grub $
Smoking:	No restrictions
Dress code:	Informal
Facilities:	Dining room; licensed lounge; banquet and conference facilities
Attractions:	Norlund chapel; Rainy River District Museum
Wheelchairs:	All public rooms and guest rooms accessible
Directions:	1 km (1/2 mile) east of Emo on Trans-Canada Highway

This is an unpretentious oasis of peace for the traveler along the (southern) Trans-Canada Highway. The Emo Inn doesn't pretend to offer gourmet dining or the most luxurious accommodation in the province, but it is comfortable and well-organized, and its staff is friendly and accommodating.

The inn comes as a pleasant surprise to the traveler tired of indifferent treatment at chain motels and hotels. The rooms are bright and clean with pastel shades and light woodwork, four-piece bathrooms, individual climate control and color TV.

The inn is only a couple of years old but it has hit its stride and sets a pleasant pace. It is included in this collection as a far-north getaway or a stepping stone between the widely spaced resort inns of the north.

The inn's dining room is light and bright, with wooden wainscoting and linen tablecloths. The dinner menu offers eight meat entrees, three beef steaks in a variety of sizes and seven fish entrees. For those who can't decide, there are four entrees combining steak and seafood. The list of eight appetizers contains offerings like Caesar salad, escargots and shrimp Barcelona.

There's a surprisingly limited dessert list of only three items, though "specialty desserts" suggests guests are invited to order their favorites custom-made. Thursday night is prime rib night, and a note on the menu suggests rare cuts would be available: "not responsible for taste or tenderness of medium well or well done meat."

This recipe from The Emo Inn is as uncomplicated as the place itself.

The Emo Inn Pepper Steak
(Serves 2)

2 oz dry sherry
4 oz beef juice
4 oz soya sauce
2 T cornstarch
4 oz cold water
1/4 cup oil

2 6-oz tenderloin steaks, cut in strips
1 green pepper, cut in strips
12 fresh mushrooms, sliced
1 small onion, sliced
6 tomato wedges

To make sauce, mix together in a small bowl sherry, beef juice, soya sauce, cornstarch and cold water.

In a wok or frying pan over high heat, heat oil. Stir fry beef quickly to sear. Add green pepper, mushrooms and onion; stir fry until colors become brilliant but vegetables are crisp. Add sauce, stirring until thickened. Add tomatoes. Serve immediately over rice.

Frenchman's Inn Restaurant

Exceptional French cuisine in a beautifully maintained 1885 Victorian-styled home setting.

Innkeepers:	Michel and Lesley Bonnot
Address:	527 Main St., Exeter, Ont. N0M 1S1
Telephone:	519-235-2008
Rooms:	No accommodation
Children:	Yes
Pets:	No
Open:	Year round, daily except Mondays. Lunch, Tues.–Fri. 11–2; Dinner, Tues.–Sun. 4–10
Food rates:	Lunch $; Dinner $$
Smoking:	No restrictions; smoke-free areas available
Dress code:	Informal
Facilities:	Fully licensed; four dining rooms; two Victorian parlors for drinks or coffee
Attractions:	Near Grand Bend's Huron Country Playhouse; zoo; beach; near Stratford Festival
Wheelchairs:	Not accessible
Directions:	On the west side of Highway 4 at the south end of Exeter

When Michel Bonnot decided to buy a fine restaurant in the heart of anglophone red-neck Ontario, he seized the bull by the proverbial horns and renamed it Frenchman's Inn. Bonnot is French, originally from Lyon. And it shows in his menus and cuisine.

The restaurant had been Robindale's Fine Dining, the second operation of the successful Robindale's of Goderich, still in operation under that name. From hefty portions of North American cuisine, Michel switched to the more subtle and versatile offerings of France.

He didn't have to do anything to the beautiful two-story yellow brick Victorian home. It had been built by Thomas Balkwell Carling, son of Isaac, one of the area's first settlers. While he opened the town's first tannery and general store, his two brothers went for the big time: they formed Carling Brewery.

The restaurant has two dining rooms on the ground floor, and its entranceway has a 25-foot ceiling. An open oak staircase leads to the second floor, where there are two parlors and a semi-private dining room for small groups.

The Frenchman's luncheon menu has a daily soup, French onion soup and lobster bisque. Starters are shrimp, smoked salmon or pâté, and there are two salads. The seven entrees cover most appetites: quiche, seafood crêpe, steak, chicken, a chef's salad with vegetables, cheese, fruit, a burger and a rolled filet of sole stuffed with salmon and saffron.

The soups and salads are the same on the dinner menu, but the starters list expands to include escargots and tartelette Neptune — a mix of crab, scallops, shrimp and mushrooms in a Newburg sauce on a light pastry shell. There are five seafood entrees and three steaks, plus veal, duck, chicken, rack of lamb and Chateaubriand. Desserts for both lunch and dinner are exotic and almost illegal, but there's a fresh fruit cup for those smitten by conscience.

Michel has offered his recipe for Terrine Maison de Foie de Volaille (in case you're having a menu printed for your next dinner party), more simply known as chicken liver pâté.

Frenchman's Chicken Liver Pâté
(Makes about 6 cups)

1 lb chicken livers
1 quart chicken stock
3/4 cup bread crumbs
4 cloves garlic, peeled and crushed
4 oz softened butter
3 eggs, beaten

1/2 cup whipping cream
2 T cognac
Salt
Freshly ground black pepper
Cayenne
Paprika

Wash and drain the livers. Simmer the stock until reduced to 1 cup; add the bread crumbs. Mix well to make a dough. Cook over low heat for 2-3 minutes; stir in the garlic.

Preheat oven to 350° F.

In a food processor, purée the livers. Add the dough and the butter, eggs, cream and cognac; season well to taste. Process until well mixed. Grease a 6-cup pan with butter and line the bottom with parchment or waxed paper. Pour the liver mixture into the pan, cover with foil and place in a shallow pan of water. Bake for 30 minutes until the pâté sets. Switch off the oven and leave pâté to cool in the oven. Refrigerate 24 hours before serving.

Benmiller Inn

A deluxe full-service country inn complex set in rolling forest land and created from three mills on Sharpes Creek and the Maitland River.

Innkeeper:	R. Peter Macaulay
Address:	R.R. 4, Goderich, Ont. N7A 3Y1
Telephone:	519-524-2191
Rooms:	48 rooms and suites all with bathroom en suite
Children:	Yes
Pets:	No
Open:	Year round. Lunch 12–2; Dinner 6–8:30; Afternoon tea 2–4:30; Sunday brunch, 11–2
Room rates:	$$$$, including continental breakfast. Off-season packages available
Food rates:	Lunch $$; Dinner $$$
Smoking:	No restrictions
Dress code:	Jacket preferred in dining room
Facilities:	Indoor heated swimming pool; sauna, whirlpool, games room; most guest rooms and public rooms overlook Sharpes Creek or the Maitland River; the inn complex is set in 75 acres of hilly, forested countryside with woodland paths and cross-country ski trails
Attractions:	Near Blyth Festival; Huron County Pioneer Museum; Huron Historic Gaol; Goderich Marine Museum

Wheelchairs:	Dining room and some guest rooms accessible
Directions:	8 km (5 miles) north of Clinton, turn right off Highway 8 onto Huron County Road 1. The inn is 3 km (2 miles) along the road.

The adjective that best describes this country retreat has traveled long and far. Port Outbound, Starboard Home was how well-heeled Brits booked their winter sea passage to warmer climes, and the acronym POSH gradually worked its way into the language to mean the best accommodation available.

That's what the guest at Benmiller gets, including an increasingly difficult-to-find commodity — peace and quiet. No sirens rip the night air in this placid crossroads, once a village whose residents operated seven mills making lumber, grain and woollen Benmiller blankets, which were a hallmark of quality far and wide.

The mills are still now and most of the villagers have moved away. Three of the mill buildings have been converted to posh rooms and suites; a frame home houses two suites and two rooms and a new building contains a conference center. There's also a recreation building with an indoor swimming pool, whirlpool, sauna, jogging track and table tennis.

Benmiller has no discotheque and there are no television sets in the rooms or suites. There are telephones, but it takes only one call to the switchboard to ensure they remain silent.

The guest rooms all have different layouts, and each is designed for maximum comfort and relaxation. Light, pastel shades of walls and floor coverings and contemporary furniture are used in many rooms, and most rooms in River Mill and Gledhill House have a private balcony or patio. Continental breakfast is included in the room rate, and guests are served fresh-baked rolls, muffins and breads in the dining room.

Here's a recipe from Benmiller's chef for one of those morning treats.

Benmiller Inn Sage Bread

(Makes 3 baguettes)

3 cups warm water
2 T sugar
4 pkg dry yeast
24 oz Bermuda onions
4 t olive oil
3 t black pepper
3 t sage
1 1/2 t salt
10 cups all purpose flour
1 egg yolk
Coarse salt and rosemary for top

Combine warm water, sugar and yeast. Let stand for 10 minutes. Sauté onions in olive oil; add black pepper and sage. Let cool. In large mixing bowl, sift together salt and flour; add yeast mixture and onion mixture. Knead until smooth dough results. Put in greased bowl and let rise in a warm place until double in bulk. Punch down and divide into three pieces. Roll into three baguettes, brush with egg yolk and sprinkle coarse salt and rosemary on top. Let rise in a warm place. Bake at 350° F for 15–20 minutes or until golden.

The Hotel Bedford

A full-service, modernized 1896 hotel on one of the corners of Goderich's unique octagonal "square."

Innkeeper:	Mike Lapaine
Address:	92 The Square, Goderich, Ont. N7A 1M2
Telephone:	519-524-7337
Rooms:	30 rooms, all with bathroom en suite
Children:	Yes
Pets:	No
Open:	Year round. 24-hour front desk service
Room rates:	$$. Off-season packages available
Food rates:	Lunch $; Dinner $$
Smoking:	No restrictions; smoke-free area available
Dress code:	Informal
Facilities:	Dining room; cocktail lounge; conference room; nightclub with dancing
Attractions:	Huron County Pioneer Museum; Huron Historic Gaol; Goderich Marine Museum; near Blyth Festival
Wheelchairs:	Dining room, lounge and nightclub accessible; guest rooms not accessible
Directions:	On the south side of The Square in downtown Goderich

Goderich is another town fortunate to have retained its downtown hotel. The Bedford has anchored one of the eight corners of the town's unique octagonal square since 1896, yet a succession of owners has kept the property in step with the times.

With an astonishing lack of tact, Queen Elizabeth II once called the city of 7,500 "the prettiest town in Canada." The town does have a fine site on a bluff overlooking Lake Huron and the valley of the Maitland River, but other equally attractive municipalities doubtless resented Her Majesty's compliment.

Goderich has the largest harbor on the Canadian side of Lake Huron, and in the shipping season visitors can count on seeing at least one laker loading grain or salt at the dock. The grain is from area farms, and the salt is mined below the waters of Lake Huron.

Dr. William "Tiger" Dunlop supervised the building of the town in 1828, naming it after Viscount Goderich, chancellor of the exchequer when the British government sold land in the Huron Tract to the Canada Company. Streets radiate from an octagonal civic park, in the center of which is the Huron County Court House.

The 1842-vintage jail is the area's premier tourist attraction, and on a hot day it's deliciously cool inside the two-foot-thick stone walls. The building is an elegant three-story octagonal structure surrounded by 20-foot-high walls separating exercise yards.

The three-story yellow brick hotel with ornate cupola faces the court house. Its ground-floor public rooms include the Duke of Bedford Cocktail Lounge, which in deference to the proximity of the court house contains a bookcase of local legalia. The Duke has a beamed ceiling and a fireplace, a loyal trade of locals, and serves diverse pub fare all day.

A wide stairway, open to the third floor of the hotel, leads to guest rooms on the second and third floors. All have recently been renovated and completely refurnished. The pine wainscoting, pine-frame beds and bathroom fixtures are all new, but each room contains at least two pieces of original furniture: wash stands, occasional chairs or dressers. The rooms are air-conditioned and there are heat lamps and oversized Hollywood-style makeup mirrors in the bathrooms.

The hotel's dining room is airy and spacious and has a nice old-fashioned feel to it. For those with a taste more modern, the hotel has built Bruno's, a New York–style nightclub with standup bar and a dance floor.

The hotel's restaurants offer a wide range of dishes, some reflecting the Italian heritage of the present owners. There are daily fish and pasta specials, the fish coming straight off the trawlers at the local harbor.

Mike has kindly made available the recipe for one of the more popular Italian dishes.

Hotel Bedford Pasta Portofino

(Serves 4)

1 16-oz package fettuccini noodles	1/4 cup diced zucchini
2 T butter	2 chicken breasts, cooked and diced
1/2 cup whipping cream	3 oz lobster or crab
Pepper	1 cup freshly grated Parmesan cheese
Crushed garlic to taste	1 large tomato, cut in 8 wedges
1/2 cup broccoli florets	2 egg yolks
1/2 cup sliced mushrooms	12 shrimp, peeled and deveined, for garnish

In large pot of boiling water, cook fettuccini until tender but firm; drain and return to pot. Meanwhile, melt butter in a large frying pan over medium heat. Add cream and bring to a simmer. Stir in pepper, crushed garlic, broccoli, mushrooms, zucchini, chicken and lobster or crab. Bring back to the simmer and add the Parmesan cheese. Add tomatoes. Add to pasta in pot, stirring gently until all strands are coated. Gently heat through, whisking in the egg yolks.

Meanwhile, fry shrimp in garlic butter. Garnish pasta with shrimp and serve immediately.

La Brassine

Some of the finest food west of Quebec is served in the elegant dining rooms of this large converted and air-conditioned farm home, which has five double guest rooms.

Innkeepers:	Tom and Nicky Blanchard-Hublet
Address:	R.R. 2, Goderich, Ont. N7A 3X8
Telephone:	519-524-6300
Rooms:	5 rooms, 4 bathrooms
Children:	Accepted if well behaved
Pets:	No
Open:	Year round. Breakfast for guests only. No lunches. Dinners served 6–8. *Note:* All dinner reservations must be made the night before with your menu choice. Dining room closed to non-guests Sunday, Monday and Tuesday
Room rates:	$$, including full English breakfast
Food rates:	Dinner $$
Smoking:	No pipes or cigars; no-smoking area available
Dress code:	Casual is acceptable, but no shorts or T-shirts
Facilities:	No liquor licence. The farm property stretches to the sandy shores of Lake Huron; large verandahs; goldfish pond
Attractions:	Near Blyth Festival, Huron Country Playhouse; Huron County Pioneer Museum; Huron Historic Gaol; Lake Huron beaches
Wheelchairs:	Not accessible
Directions:	Off Highway 21 midway between Bayfield and Goderich. Turn west (towards the lake) on Kitchigami Road; the inn is on the first driveway on the right.

Dinner reservations at La Brassine must be made 24 hours in advance, and at that time guests can select their dishes, unless they are having the four-course meal of the day. This allows the diner more time to make a lot of difficult decisions when confronted with a menu that reads like the What's What of gastronomic tantalizers.

Before my wife and I booked a dinner with friends at La Brassine, we spent a week with a copy of the four-page menu. Each evening we drooled over it and each evening we changed the choices we had made the previous night. By the time that long-awaited dinner arrived our menu was dog-eared and we had deliberately avoided lunch. The agonizing really hadn't been necessary; all the dishes were superb. It may upset some innkeepers whose establishments are also listed in this guide, but that meal was the finest restaurant meal I have ever been served in Ontario.

Many of the dishes are from Nicky's native Belgium, but there are also surprises on the menu gathered from her travels with Tom to the far corners of the world. Their living room and the dining rooms are museums of fine china, crystal, silver pieces and other art objects accumulated during those travels.

Nicky holds sway in her huge kitchen, and Tom serves diners at linen-covered tables set with crystal and silver. Everything served is created in-house, from salad dressings to cakes and pastries. The light background classical music doesn't intrude on conversation.

Guest rooms on the upper two floors are comfortable and have all just been refurbished at the same time the house was air-conditioned. The rooms overlook farm fields, a garden and goldfish pond, and those at the front have a glimpse, through huge trees, of Lake Huron.

Following is a recipe for one favorite from La Brassine's menu.

La Brassine Poulet Sauté à la Provençale

(Serves 4–6)

3 1/2–4 lb chicken, cut in 8 pieces
8 sprigs fresh thyme
8 large slices of Canadian bacon
1/4 cup butter
5–6 T olive oil
1 large onion, chopped
4 tomatoes, skinned, seeded and slivered
1 1/2 t flour
1 1/2 cups dry white wine
1 clove garlic, crushed
Salt and pepper to taste
8 slices French bread
Parsley, finely chopped

Place a sprig of thyme on each piece of chicken, wrap with a slice of bacon and secure with string. Heat butter and oil in heavy pan over medium-high heat. Fry chicken until nicely browned all over. Remove from pan. Add the onion and tomatoes to pan, cook until soft (*but not brown*). Pour off surplus fat; add flour and mix well. Pour on the wine, garlic and salt and pepper. Bring to the boil. Replace the chicken, cover, and simmer very gently, 30–45 minutes, or until tender.

Meanwhile, in a separate pan over medium heat, fry French bread slices in oil until golden brown.

Remove chicken from pan, remove string from chicken pieces, and place chicken in warm serving dish. Reduce the cooking liquid until it is the consistency of thick cream; pour over the chicken. Garnish the dish with the fried French bread and generously sprinkle with parsley. Serve immediately.

Olde Heidelberg Brewery and Restaurant

A country party brew pub with honky-tonk piano sing alongs, basic motel accommodation and huge servings of great, reasonably priced food.

Innkeepers:	Howie and Bob MacMillan
Address:	2 King St., Heidelberg, Ont. N0B 1Y0
Telephone:	519-699-4413
Rooms:	16, all with bathroom en suite
Children:	Yes
Pets:	Yes
Open:	Year round. Mon.-Thurs. 11-midnight; Fri. & Sat. 11-1; Sun. noon-8
Room rates:	$
Food rates:	Dinner $; Daily dinner special $; Pub grub $; child's portion 50% plus $1
Dress code:	Come as you are
Smoking:	No restrictions
Facilities:	Honky-tonk piano; pool tables; shuffleboards
Attractions:	In the heart of Mennonite country near the attractions of Kitchener
Wheelchairs:	All areas and motel accessible
Directions:	In the village of Heidelberg, 10 km (6 miles) northwest of Waterloo

A small brass plaque just inside the front door sets the tone for your evening at this party place. "On this site in 1897," it reads, "nothing happened."

Then you're inside the 1838 tavern, which is the largest industry in this rural crossroads whose population is listed at 500. You can't call Heidelberg a one-horse town because every few minutes you'll see horses strutting through the village hauling Mennonite families in their distinctive black buggies.

Inside the tavern is a truly eclectic mix of clientele. At one table you may see Mom and Dad and the kiddies all dressed up and treating Grandmother to a night out. They're the sort of family that wouldn't normally set foot in a licensed establishment and are pointedly ordering soft drinks, tea and coffee.

The nearby tables are occupied by yuppies letting their hair down. They've chartered a bus and are doing a rural pub tour; some of them look as though this may be their second day on the road. Back in the corner some bearded locals wearing ball caps are raucously appreciating an off-color joke.

The two pool tables and two shuffleboard tables have lineups, and others crowd the stand-up bar waiting for tables. Waiters and waitresses scurry through the crowd with the trademark platters heaped with ribs, pig tails, Wiener schnitzels, sauerkraut and hot apple turnovers.

There's a brisk trade in O.B., a Bavarian lager brewed on the premises that is sweeter than brews from domestic breweries and has a more hoppy flavor. It contains no preservatives and is served unpasteurized.

That family group looking askance at the occupants of the neighboring tables may not enjoy the tobacco smoke or the occasional noisy party. And they certainly disapprove of the gallonage of O.B. that's disappearing around them. But they're regulars, too. They're here for the food, which has earned a far-flung reputation and is one of the area's best deals.

The MacMillans have kindly shared the recipe for one of their most popular dishes, chef Violet Rank's recipe for pig tails.

Olde Heidelberg Pig Tails
(Serves 12)

8–10 lbs pig tails
2 cups 7-Up
6 cups brown sugar
3 T prepared mustard
1 rounded T cloves
1 rounded T curry powder
1 rounded T allspice

In a 350° F oven, roast pig tails for 1 1/2 hours. Combine remaining ingredients and mix thoroughly into a juice. Pour juice over tails and roast another 1 1/2 hours, or until meat is tender.

Grandview Inn

A full-service luxury resort in the heart of Muskoka with a tradition of hospitality reaching back to 1874.

Innkeeper:	Randy Cooper
Address:	R.R. 4, Huntsville, Ont. P0A 1K0
Telephone:	705-789-4417
Rooms:	154 rooms and suites
Children:	Yes
Pets:	No
Open:	Year round. Lunch 11:30–2:30; Dinner 5:30–10; Sunday brunch 10:30–3
Room rates:	$$$$$$. Variety of packages available
Food rates:	Lunch $; Dinner $$$
Smoking:	Smoke-free section available
Dress code:	Country casual
Facilities:	Fully licensed dining room; pub; billiards; meeting rooms with audio-visual equipment; indoor swimming pool, sauna, whirlpool, exercise room, outdoor swimming pool, indoor and outdoor tennis courts, croquet, badminton, volleyball, mountain bikes, cross-country skiing, skating rink

Attractions:	Near Muskoka Pioneer Village; Madill Church; Lion's Lookout Park; Dyer Memorial; Hidden Valley ski area; Algonquin Park
Wheelchairs:	All public rooms and some guest rooms accessible
Directions:	On Highway 60 about 2 km (1 1/4 miles) east of Huntsville

One of the resort's brochures boasts: "The only things we overlook are the lake, the golf course, the tennis courts . . ." And the boast is true. The deluxe rooms and suites of Grandview also overlook a lovely slice of Muskoka, a part of Ontario that enjoys four distinctive seasons. The seasons are clearly delineated in this snow zone where winter is winter and there's no confusion about it as there so often is in the south.

Grandview's hospitality history goes back to 1874, but the only remnant of that era is the small inn overlooking Fairy Lake and now one of the dining rooms. The rooms and suites are modern and equipped with all conveniences. The suites have fully equipped kitchens, dining rooms, fireplaces, whirlpool baths and large decks overlooking Fairy Lake or the resort's own nine-hole golf course.

The resort is designed to accommodate business seminars and meetings and has all the executive toys for those as well as complete sports and relaxation facilities. Other guests can enjoy the recreation facilities and fine dining . . . without having to attend the business meetings.

Casual dining is available at Dockside Restaurant, but a more elegant environment is the spacious original inn, which has been converted for dining.

The menu is extensive and the desserts are sinful. Here's the recipe for one popular entree.

Grandview Chicken Grand Marnier

(Serves 2)

2 oz white wine
1 oz butter
2 6-oz chicken breasts
2 oz Grand Marnier
1 t sweet orange marmalade

1 t orange zest
1 cup 35% cream
Salt and white pepper to taste
Orange segments for garnish

Preheat oven to 350° F.

In a large oven-proof frying pan, heat wine and butter; add chicken breasts. Place pan in oven and bake for 10–15 minutes or until chicken is tender. Remove chicken. Over high heat, reduce cooking liquid by 3/4. Deglaze pan with Grand Marnier, marmalade and zest. Reduce again. Add cream and reduce until sauce thickens. Season chicken with salt and white pepper to taste. Place chicken on dinner plates, spoon sauce over, and garnish with segments of orange.

Norsemen Restaurant

Fine continental cuisine with a European flair in an 1870 building with stone fireplaces on the shores of Walker Lake.

Innkeepers:	Lynda and Enno Kerckhoff
Address:	Old Limberlost Rd., R.R. 4, Huntsville, Ont. P0A 1K0
Telephone:	705-635-2473
Rooms:	6 two-bedroom lakeside cottages with fully equipped kitchens; 1 three-bedroom cottage
Children:	Yes
Pets:	No
Open:	Year round. July & Aug., Lunch 11–2, Dinner from 5:30. May, June, Sept., Oct., Dinner only, Wed.–Sun. from 6 p.m. Nov.–Apr., Dinner only, Thur.–Sun. from 6 p.m.
Cottage rates:	$400–$600 per person per week. Weekend rates available fall through spring
Food rates:	Lunch $; Dinner $$
Smoking:	Smoke-free section available
Dress code:	Casual
Facilities:	Fully licensed dining room with two wood-burning fireplaces; fishing, canoeing, boating on Walker Lake (no jet skis or water skiing)

Attractions: In beautiful Muskoka; hiking, canoeing, cross-country and alpine skiing; Muskoka Pioneer Village; Madill Church; Lion's Lookout Park; near championship golf course (Deerhurst) and several others open to the public
Wheelchairs: All public rooms and two cottages accessible
Directions: Take Highway 60 about 10 km (6 miles) east of Huntsville. Turn north on Limberlost Rd. (Muskoka Regional Road 8). Take turning to left after about 2 km (1 1/4 miles).

The original 1870 home was converted to Royal Oak Lodge in 1920 and remained a lodge until 1977, when it became a restaurant. Lynda and Enno bought the property in 1989, got chef de cuisine Raymond McGuire on their team and began to establish a reputation for fine dining.

Each of two dining areas has a massive stone fireplace, the original hand-hewn ceiling beams and Axminster carpeting for added warmth. A cozy lodge surrounded by virgin bush isn't the sort of place you'd expect to find dishes like pork tenderloin Franjelico on the dinner menu — that's a tenderloin stuffed with figs, roasted and served in a white wine and Franjelico cream sauce, garnished with hazelnuts.

And that isn't Chef Raymond's only surprise on the nine-entree menu, which has imaginative appetizers: how about paupiettes of pasta stuffed with shrimp and scallops, poached in white wine, garlic, soya and ginger and served with a white wine butter sauce?

A third dining area is available for up to eight diners who must reserve it at least a week in advance. This is The Chef's Table, completely separated from the main dining rooms. Here gourmands may enjoy a custom-designed menu of up to seven courses of very special dishes.

The cottages all face small Walker Lake, which yields good bass. When the lake is frozen it's a daily occurrence to see herds of 20 or 30 deer cross it to feeding stations on either side.

Five of the cottages are "traditional Muskoka" in design and construction. They were built in the mid-1930s and have pine floors and pine tongue-and-groove ceilings. The older cottages have all modern conveniences but have not yet been winterized. The other two are modern Viceroy cottages with cedar siding and fireplaces.

Chef Raymond has kindly shared his own unique recipe for vinaigrette dressing.

Norsemen Muskoka Cranberry Vinaigrette Dressing

1 orange
1/2 lemon
4 cups water
1 cup white vinegar

3/4 cup white sugar
Pinch salt
1 10-oz pkg fresh or frozen cranberries
2 cups vegetable or olive oil

Into a large stainless steel pot, squeeze the oranges and lemon. Add the water, vinegar, sugar, salt and cranberries. Simmer 2–3 hours, stirring periodically (and savor the aroma!). When the mixture has been reduced by one-half, let it cool to room temperature. Refrigerate a minimum of 48 hours to allow flavors to mingle and mellow.

Strain the mixture through a very fine sieve or press through cheesecloth. Blend in the (best quality) vegetable or olive oil. Before serving, whisk or stir the vinaigrette thoroughly. Serve over assorted leaves or salads.

Elm Hurst Inn

A luxurious, full-service country inn with fine dining. One dining area dates to 1872.

Innkeepers:	Margaret and Gerald Ball
Address:	P.O. Box 123, Ingersoll, Ont. N5C 3K1
Telephone:	519-485-5321
Rooms:	49 rooms and suites, all with bathroom en suite
Children:	Yes
Pets:	No
Open:	Year round. Lunch noon–2; Dinner, Mon.–Sat. 5–9; Sunday brunch 10:30–2; Sunday dinner 4–8
Room rates:	$$$$
Food rates:	Lunch $; Dinner $$;
Smoking:	In designated areas
Dress code:	Jacket preferred in dining rooms
Facilities:	Eleven Victorian-style dining rooms; James Harris Café; meeting rooms; wedding facilities; specialty boutiques and gallery of local crafts
Attractions:	Near Ingersoll Golf and Country Club; Ingersoll Cheese Museum; Coyle's of Tillsonburg
Wheelchairs:	All guest rooms and some dining rooms accessible
Directions:	Just north of Highway 401 at Exit 218B (Highway 19)

When cheese baron James Harris built his mansion just south of Ingersoll in 1872, it was a class act. So when Margaret and Gerald Ball announced in 1987 that they were building a 49-room annex to their restaurant complex, folks assumed this would also be a class act.

What the Balls did, however, was put their class act into a class all by itself.

"We didn't want to copy the original building," Margaret explains. "That would have been a forgery. We wanted to complement it." And complement it they did. The result resembles a European chateau rearing up from the gentle undulations of Southwestern Ontario farm country. The distinctive architecture of the new section complements the original and the original complements the new; a perfect marriage.

Rooms and suites in the three-story addition are large and decorated in one of four color schemes. All rooms have a desk and chair, table and two comfortable chairs; the furniture is oak with a cherry finish. Rooms on the third floor have brass chandeliers in dormers with cathedral ceilings.

Behind the original Harris home, a nineteenth-century barn has obtained a new lease on life by being converted to a craft shop, boutiques and a gallery. The Carriage House features local crafts and is well stocked with tasteful, off-beat gift items.

The lunch menu has a range for a variety of appetites from light to heavy, or a buffet including hot entrees. The dinner menu has a dozen entrees and a daily three-course special. (A note beneath the Chateaubriand for two indicates that the chef not only takes quality seriously but has the support of management as well. The note reads: "No well done please.")

One of Elm Hurst's trademarks has become the seven-course Hunt Feast for two, which requires at least 24 hours' notice. Chef Wayne Zavitz has offered his recipe for one of the particularly popular Elm Hurst menu items.

Elm Hurst Herbed Chicken Fromage with Lemon and Dill Sauce

(Serves 6)

6 6-oz boneless chicken breasts

6 1-oz cubes herbed cream cheese

Sauce

5 egg yolks

20 oz clarified butter

4 oz white wine

Salt and white pepper

Lemon juice

Dill weed, crushed

Preheat oven to 350° F.

In a large frying pan, fry chicken until it is cooked halfway through. Cut a small slit lengthwise in each breast and place one cube of cheese inside each breast. Bake chicken on a greased pan for 15 minutes or until cooked.

To make the sauce: In a blender or food processor, mix egg yolks and butter, 1 yolk and 4 oz butter at a time. Blend until thick. Add wine and blend more. Add salt and white pepper, lemon juice and dill weed to taste. Serve at room temperature, poured over chicken.

The Queen's Inn

An appealing 17-room early Canadian inn in an 1839 limestone and brick landmark of this historic city. North American cuisine; sports pub.

Innkeepers:	Richard Mitchell, Kathy Cornell, Ruby and Ron Mitchell
Address:	125 Brock St., Kingston, Ont. K7L 1S1
Telephone:	613-546-0429
Rooms:	17 rooms and suites all with bathroom en suite
Children:	Yes
Pets:	No
Open:	Year round, daily 11 a.m.–1 a.m.; food service until 10 p.m.
Room rates:	$$, including continental breakfast
Food rates:	Lunch $; Dinner $
Smoking:	No restrictions
Dress code:	Casual
Facilities:	Coppers Good Eats Restaurant, serving salads, burgers and steaks, extends outside to Brock St. in summer; The Sports, with free popcorn and wide-screen TV, has a pub grub menu
Attractions:	Old Fort Henry; boat tours; Marine Museum; Agnes Etherington Art Centre; Bellevue House; historic City Hall; Maclachlan Woodworking Museum; Royal Military College Museum; Pump House Steam Museum

Wheelchairs: Not accessible
Directions: In downtown Kingston. From Highway 401 take Division St. Exit, follow Princess St. 4 km (2 1/2 miles), turn right on Wellington St. and right on Brock St.

The big change at the venerable Queen's Inn came in 1987. That's when the Mitchells converted 24 tiny rooms to 17 modern air-conditioned guest rooms with four-piece bathrooms en suite. The rooms are light and bright, and the new furniture is Canadian antique reproductions in maple. All rooms on the third floor have skylights.

The sports bar draws fans of baseball, soccer, boxing, wrestling and hockey. Its menu has a long list of pub grub from salads through steaks, from finger food to sandwiches made of kaiser rolls and garnished with slaw and chunky french fries.

The fully licensed Coppers Good Eats is more a pub than a dining room. Bar stools surround a square bar that dispenses six brands of draft beer. It's bright and spacious, and the most popular dishes are burgers, hot sandwiches and fish and chips — an extension, really, of the sports bar pub menu. The place is informal; service is friendly and fast. In summer Coppers extends out to a sidewalk patio with small tables shaded by umbrellas.

Richard Mitchell has offered the recipe for one of the Queen's Inn's favorite menu items, scaled for a large group. The recipe quantities can easily be reduced for home use.

Queen's Inn Chile Con Carne

(Serves the whole gang — and then some!)

10 lb lean ground beef	1 T paprika
5 stalks celery, chopped	1 T garlic powder
2 large Spanish onions, chopped	1 T crushed red chilies
2 green peppers, chopped	100-oz can crushed tomatoes
1/4 cup chili powder	100-oz can red kidney beans

In your biggest pot, dump everything except the beans and tomatoes. Cook slowly until the vegetables are soft and translucent. Drain excess fat. Add the crushed tomatoes and kidney beans. Simmer for half an hour.

Walper Terrace Hotel

A Kitchener landmark sensitively restored to its 1893 Victorian elegance. Two dining rooms, mini shopping mall and all the amenities of a first-class small city hotel.

Innkeeper:	Sobhy El-Ganzoury
Address:	One King St. West, Kitchener, Ont. N2G 1A1
Telephone:	519-745-4321
Rooms:	112 rooms, including 19 suites, all with bathroom en suite
Children:	Yes
Pets:	No
Open:	Year round. Sunday brunch 10:30–2:30
Room rates:	$$$. Off-season packages available
Food rates:	Lunch $; Dinner $$
Smoking:	In designated areas
Dress code:	Jacket preferred in dining rooms
Facilities:	Two distinctly different dining areas; lounge; several shops on the ground floor; ballroom; meeting rooms

Attractions: A stroll from Farmers' Market, the Glockenspiel and Centre in the Square; near Joseph Schneider House, Seagram Museum, Bingeman Park, Doon Heritage Crossroads, Homer Watson Gallery, Lulu's Roadhouse, Sportsworld, Woodside National Historic Site and home of the Kitchener-Waterloo Oktoberfest
Wheelchairs: All public rooms and some guest rooms accessible
Directions: In downtown Kitchener at the corner of King and Queen streets

The rejuvenated Walper Terrace Hotel sustains a Kitchener tradition started in 1820 by Phineas Varnum. Back then, when the community was known as Sandhills, Varnum leased land from Joseph Schneider (of packing-house fame) and built the Varnum Inn. Behind the inn, Varnum built a log cabin in which Mennonite immigrants could stay free of charge until they finished building their own homes.

The inn underwent a number of additions before it was destroyed by fire in 1892. The following year the existing four stories of the hotel were built on the site and in 1925 the Crystal ballroom and two more floors were added. The hotel's original elegance was restored during extensive renovations in 1984.

No detail was overlooked. The Art Deco terrazzo floor of the Terrace Café was restored along with wooden moldings, carved marble pillars and the ornate brass bannister of the main staircase.

The Terrace Café is one of the most popular dining spots in town. It has vaulted ceilings, marble pillars, stained glass windows and a street-level view of one of the city's main downtown intersections — a perfect place for people-watching. La Galleria Restaurant is decorated in Mediterranean motif, has an extensive menu of Italian cuisine and a dress code for diners.

The recipe offered by the Walper is another Kitchener tradition; it has been on the hotel's menu for decades and has been revised by chef Carlos Reyes.

Walper Terrace Spinach Salad à la Chef Carlos

1 bag fresh spinach
1/2 cup frozen raspberries
1/2 cup vegetable oil
2 oz red wine vinegar

1 t Dijon mustard
2 t Tabasco sauce
Sprinkle of lemon juice
1 t Worcestershire sauce

Garnishes
Chopped fresh parsley
Finely chopped onion
Chopped fresh basil
Garlic croutons

Toasted almonds
Mandarin orange segments
Baby shrimps (optional)

Wash and stem spinach, wrap in dry towel and place in refrigerator. Combine raspberries, vegetable oil, vinegar, mustard, Tabasco, lemon juice and Worcestershire sauce and blend until creamy. Toss spinach and dressing in a large glass bowl. Top with garnishes.

Fisherman's Wharf Restaurant and Motel

The pub is a social center for locals and visitors, and a deck overlooking Big Head River extends the dining room for summer lunches and dinners.

Innkeepers:	Lee and Gary Skrepnek
Address:	12 Bayfield St., P.O. Box 374, Meaford, Ont. N0H 1Y0
Telephone:	519-538-1390
Rooms:	8 motel units, 6 of which are efficiency units, some accommodating up to six people, all with bathroom en suite
Children:	Yes
Pets:	Yes
Open:	Year round. Pub, 11–12; Dining room, 11–9
Room rates:	$. Off-season packages available
Food rates:	Lunch $; Dinner $; Pub grub $
Smoking:	No restrictions
Dress code:	Informal
Facilities:	Pub with games, dart boards; fully licensed dining room and patio overlooking Big Head River where it empties into Meaford Harbour off Nottawasaga Bay, an inlet of Georgian Bay

Attractions: Rainbow fishing at your doorstep; Meaford Museum; near Collingwood for winter skiing and summer Great Slide Ride; active community theater; ice fishing
Wheelchairs: Only motel units are accessible
Directions: At the bridge on Bayfield St. where Big Head River empties into Meaford Harbour near the marina

The food isn't gourmet and the motel units aren't Ontario's most opulent, but Fisherman's Wharf is a pleasant, comfortable place where the visitor quickly feels at home and at ease.

The town of Meaford is a comfortable place, too. It has a small opera house and active theater group, it welcomes skiers and ice fishermen in winter, boaters in summer and fishermen from spring through autumn.

Many of those visitors make the pub at Fisherman's Wharf their local. Its proper name is the St. Vincent Arms Pub, a name that reflects a bit of the town's history. The community was first known as Stephenson's Landing, after the first innkeeper. It was later renamed for Meaford Hall, the Staffordshire estate of Admiral Sir John Jervis, Earl St. Vincent, after whom the surrounding township of St. Vincent is named.

The menu of Fisherman's Wharf Restaurant reflects its location in a Great Lakes fishing port. Whitefish (the world-record fish was caught just offshore) and splake are on both the lunch and dinner menus, and one of the daily specials is catch of the day. There's also a daily dinner special and daily pasta special.

Not surprisingly, one of the recipes the Skrepneks have kindly made available is for seafood.

Fisherman's Wharf Crab and Baby Shrimp Crêpes

(Serves 2)

1 1/2 cups 18% cream
4 mushrooms, sliced
1 t garlic, puréed
Salt and white pepper to taste

6 oz crab meat
4 oz cooked baby shrimp
1/4 cup grated Parmesan cheese
2 crêpes

In a saucepan over medium heat, bring cream to a boil. Add mushrooms, garlic and salt and white pepper; simmer 2–3 minutes. Add crab and baby shrimp; simmer 1–2 minutes. Add Parmesan cheese; blend in thoroughly. Pour about half the mixture on each crêpe, reserving some to spoon on top. Fold over crêpes and spoon remaining mixture on top. (Serve with rice pilaf and sautéed zucchini or steamed broccoli.)

Herigate Inn

A quiet, unpretentious hotel/motel near Toronto and Hamilton airports with lounge and reasonably priced dining room.

Innkeeper:	John Vranich
Address:	161 Chisholm Dr., Milton, Ont. L9T 4A6
Telephone:	416-878-2825
Rooms:	77 rooms, including 2 suites and a honeymoon suite
Children:	Yes
Pets:	Yes
Open:	Year round. 24-hour front desk service. Dining room: Mon.-Fri. 6-10, Sat. 8-10, Sun. 8-9
Room rates:	$$$. Weekend packages available
Food rates:	Lunch $; Dinner $$
Smoking:	No restrictions; smoke-free area available
Dress code:	Informal
Facilities:	Dining room; licensed patio and lounge; outdoor heated pool; news-stand/gift shop
Attractions:	Near Ontario Agricultural Museum; Canada's Wonderland; Crawford Lake Conservation Area; Halton Region Museum; Mohawk Raceway; Mountsberg Wildlife Centre
Wheelchairs:	Dining room, lounge, patio and 2 guest rooms accessible
Directions:	From Highway 401, take Highway 25 south (Exit 320A). At the first traffic light, Chisholm Dr., turn right and follow for 0.4 km (1/4 mile).

You can see the inn from Highway 401. The five-story hotel section sticks up in the middle of a field and you can clearly see the large sign bearing the inn's name. From the highway it looks as though the Herigate is in the middle of nowhere.

When you make the effort to get to it, you find a pleasant little self-contained oasis removed from the hurly-burly of Toronto and the frenzied pace of Highway 401. Some city people in the know use the inn as their weekend hideaway when they want a breath of country air and don't want to spend a lot of time driving there and back.

The guest rooms are well maintained, furnished in oak and have extra-long beds with low-mileage mattresses. There's color cable TV with in-room movies.

Tropics Piano Bar ought to have a strong local following because it's an attractive little bar, but it isn't always open. Another bar off the dining room does keep regular hours, so the guest is never stuck without a drink or friendly bartender to chat with on a slow night.

The dining room, Original Hickory's, has lots of greenery, ceiling fans and colorful stonework. Service is friendly and informal. The lunch menu has interesting options as well as a daily special, daily pasta special, quiche of the day and soup of the day. There are light dishes like crêpes Louise, light crêpes filled with seafood and topped with Hollandaise, or Ryan's salad, a complete meal of diced chicken breast, pineapple, fresh vegetables and lettuce tossed in a light dressing.

Dinner offerings include a grilled chicken breast marinated in lemon juice with a hint of garlic, and pork medallions sautéed in white wine with peaches and herbs.

Chef Keith Waters has given us the recipe for one of the inn's popular lunch and dinner entrees, which, he says, takes only 15 minutes to prepare.

Herigate Tarragon Chicken

(Serves 4)

4 large chicken breasts, skinned and de-boned
2 oz clarified butter
3 oz white wine
Tarragon leaves to taste
2 cups 35% cream
Salt and pepper to taste

Preheat oven to 350° F.

In large frying pan, sauté breasts in butter until cooked halfway through. Remove chicken to a baking dish and bake for 15 minutes or until cooked. Meanwhile, deglaze pan with wine. Add tarragon and reduce; add cream and reduce. Stir in salt and pepper. Serve chicken on a bed of rice with sauce poured over.

The Heritage Inn

An 1840 octagonal home with eight gables, cleverly converted to a bright, spacious country dining establishment serving lunch and dinner.

Innkeeper:	Heidi Dittrich
Address:	P.O. Box 65, Mount Pleasant, Ont. N0E 1K0
Telephone:	519-484-2551
Rooms:	No accommodation
Children:	Yes
Open:	Year round, Tues.-Fri. and Sun. Lunch 11:30-2:30; Dinner 5-10; Sunday brunch 11-2, Dinner 5-9
Food rates:	Lunch $; Dinner $
Smoking:	In designated areas
Dress code:	Informal
Facilities:	Private banquet room available
Attractions:	Near Alexander Graham Bell Homestead; Rev. Thomas Henderson Museum; Brant County Museum; Glenhyrst Art Gallery of Brant; Her Majesty's Royal Chapel of the Mohawks; Chiefswood; Myrtleville House Museum; Woodland Cultural Centre; Sanderson Centre for the Performing Arts; ICOMM (Interaction Communications Centre); Adelaide Hunter-Hoodless Homestead Museum; Big Creek Boat Farm

Wheelchairs: Not accessible
Directions: 5 km (3 miles) south of Brantford on Mount Pleasant Rd. (old Highway 24)

If you don't have time for lunch or dinner, at least stop in for coffee or a drink. This unique building is a delight to visit. There are perhaps half a dozen octagonal homes across Ontario, but none with eight gables.

This one was built in 1840 by well-heeled Scottish shoemaker Richard Tennant. Before it was converted into a restaurant in 1974, it had been the home of a number of families, a Royal Canadian Legion branch and an apartment building.

Now it's a beautiful place for dining, with high windows and an octagonal glassed cupola pouring light through the high main dining room onto the tables. There's a huge stone fireplace, and the walls are lined with old photographs, animal skins and heads, and bits of antique Canadiana. For additional privacy, dine in one of the cozy eaves off the second-floor galleria.

The lunch menu is international; entrees range from veal piccata through a New York steak and chicken stir-fry to Cajun catfish. There's a daily pasta special. The dinner menu expands to 13 entrees with something for every taste and appetite, from Chateaubriand for two to orange roughy flambéed in Pernod and orange sauce.

Chef Michael Safko has kindly offered to share this recipe for his popular treatment of roasted rack of lamb.

Heritage Inn Roasted Rack of Lamb

(Serves 2)

2 racks of lamb	*4 tomatoes*
Dijon mustard	*1 oz fresh mint, chopped*
2 T cooking oil	*1 1/2 oz white wine*
1 clove garlic, chopped	*Salt and pepper to taste*

Preheat oven to 350° F.

Coat the lamb with Dijon mustard. Heat cooking oil in an oven-proof frying pan over medium-high heat; add the garlic and the lamb; fry the lamb on both sides until brown. Place in oven for 15 minutes. (This will cook it to medium.) Meanwhile, skin the tomatoes by dropping them in boiling water for about 10 seconds. Cut in half and remove seeds. In blender or food processor, purée tomatoes, chopped mint and 1 oz wine.

When the lamb is cooked, remove from pan and drain off the grease. Deglaze the pan with remaining 1/2 oz wine. Add tomato-mint sauce to pan; heat and season to taste. Cut the racks into single chops, arrange evenly on a plate and serve with sauce on the side or over the lamb.

If fresh mint is not available, mint sauce will do, but use only 1/2 ounce of wine in tomato-mint purée.

The Great British Emporium

A country tea room that also serves lunches in the pretty village of New Dundee. Visitors can browse a number of rooms of antiques, curios and gift items.

Innkeepers:	Gail Groen and Judy Luft
Address:	169 Front St., New Dundee, Ont. N0B 2E0
Telephone:	519-696-2223
Rooms:	No accommodation
Children:	Yes
Open:	Year round. Tues.–Sat. & holiday Mondays 10–6; Sun. 11–6. Tea room closes at 5 p.m.; gift shop open until 6 p.m.
Food rates:	Lunch $; Tea $
Smoking:	Smoking room available
Dress code:	Come as you are
Facilities:	Fully licensed dining room
Attractions:	A wonderful potpourri of old and new gift items; New Dundee is a pretty hamlet between the attractions of Kitchener and Brantford
Wheelchairs:	Tea room and downstairs store area accessible
Directions:	On the main street of the village. From Highway 7 & 8 take the well-marked New Dundee cutoff (Regional Road 12). From Highway 401, take Exit 34 (New Dundee Road).

This quaint step back to an era of fewer pressures and a less frantic lifestyle is worth the detour from Highways 401 or 7 & 8 for a leisurely lunch of real food or afternoon tea. Yes, you can have a cold beer, a glass of wine or a liqueur, since The Emporium is fully licensed.

If your teenagers are along, you may have to help them with the handwritten menu: there are no chili dogs or hamburgers, but there are wonderful things like savory pie, ploughman's lunch, quiche with seasonal garnish, and seafood salad.

The house pâté, flavored with herbs and sherry, is served with Scottish oatcakes, and the daily soup comes with oatmeal bread baked on the premises.

Afternoon tea is not for the weak-willed who had difficulty fitting into trousers or a skirt that morning. The traditional Scottish cream tea is accompanied by warm scones with butter, preserves and Devon cream. Or there are toasted crumpets, warm shortbreads and raspberry and rhubarb pie. Going for broke? Try the Boozy Cheesecake or Belgian Chocolate Mousse Cake.

The tea/lunch room is at the rear of a Victorian country general store that still has its 1887 wood floors, counters and shelves. The browser weaves between counters and racks and stands of knick-knacks, gadgets, preserves, books, cards, brassware, leather goods, scarves, toys — all sorts of special, and mostly quality, items that could knock a lot of names off your Christmas list in the middle of July.

Upstairs there are more rooms of cuddly toys, books, antiques, bits and pieces of furniture and odds and ends. This is no place to bring an Olympic-class shopper (if you're picking up his/her tab).

Gail and Judy have passed along the recipe for their scones, noting that to achieve perfection requires being a good cook to start with and then having lots of practice.

Great British Emporium Scones

(Makes about 5 dozen; the scone mix
may be frozen and the baked scones may be frozen)

20 cups all purpose flour
8 cups whole wheat flour
2 2/3 cups granulated sugar

1 cup plus 1 T baking powder
5 t salt
2 pounds margarine

Mix the dry ingredients in a large basin. Cream the margarine and work into dry ingredients until mixture resembles coarse crumbs.

To make scones:
1 1/2 cups buttermilk
1 1/2 cups milk

8 cups scone mix
1 egg, beaten

Preheat oven to 425° F.

Add buttermilk and milk to scone mix. Mix lightly and knead 8 to 10 times to form a soft dough. On a floured surface, roll out to about 1-inch thickness. Cut scones with a 2 1/2-inch cutter. Put on cookie sheet 2 inches apart and brush with beaten egg. Bake 10 minutes. Turn the pan and bake an additional 4–5 minutes or until lightly browned. Place pans on a rack to cool.

At The Emporium the scones are served with butter, preserves, Devon cream and British tea.

The Waterlot Restaurant

Fine continental cuisine with attentive, professional service in four cozy rooms and the glassed-in patio of a stately 1846 home on the banks of the Nith River.

Innkeeper:	Gord Elkeer
Address:	17 Huron St., P.O. Box 1077, New Hamburg, Ont. N0B 2G0
Telephone:	519-662-2020
Rooms:	2 large rooms sharing bathroom; 1 suite with bathroom en suite
Children:	No
Pets:	No
Open:	Year round, daily except Mondays. Lunch 11:30–2; Dinner from 5 p.m.; Sunday brunch 11 & 1:30
Room rates:	$$, including continental breakfast
Food rates:	Lunch $; Dinner $$
Smoking:	No cigars or pipes in dining room
Dress code:	Casual
Facilities:	Five distinctly different dining rooms, two with wood-burning fireplaces; Le Bistro, a glass-enclosed patio, overlooks the Nith River, which meanders through the back yard

Attractions:	Selfhelp Crafts Canada outlet; Riverside Brass, Canada's largest brassware outlet; gourmet food and gift shop next door
Wheelchairs:	Dining room and patio accessible; guest rooms not accessible
Directions:	At Huron and Wilmot streets in the heart of New Hamburg, behind the Royal Bank

In winter try for a table near the crackling fireplace; in summer try for one near the picture windows overlooking the Nith River and Waterwheel Park. There are lush green lawns shaded by huge willow trees that lined the millrace, which was filled in a few decades ago.

The Waterlot is a primrose yellow-brick building whose architectural style doesn't fit handily into any category. It's mostly Victorian, but an elegant cupola sits atop the main roof ridge, giving the building an Italian flavor. The cupola is surrounded by a widow's walk, and gingerbread decorates the eaves.

William J. Scott, also known as Lord Campfield, built the house after he bought the community's first mill and the water rights. He went on to be the first postmaster, reeve of the township and operator of a cloth factory, flour mill, sawmill, general store and distillery. (To break up a romance between his daughter and a local suitor of whom he obviously disapproved, Scott moved his family to New Zealand.)

The Waterlot is a pretty building that invites entry, and its dining rooms lend themselves to a leisurely lunch or dinner. The restaurant has developed a loyal following over the years, which didn't happen just because the building is so attractive.

The kitchen uses only fresh produce, local and organic when possible, sweet butter, non-fat skim milk, whole grain flour and yogurt, fresh fruits and herbs. No additives are used and dishes have a low sodium content. Any who wonder what sort of fare they'll be served can browse the impressive array of culinary awards framed in the front parlor.

The baked goods are produced in the restaurant's kitchen, and some of the most popular dessert items are sold in a gourmet food shop next door, called The Waterlot Store. It's a good place to look for those hard-to-find ingredients, cooking aids and gift items.

The two large guest rooms are in the two peaks at the front of the house. They share a sitting area lighted by the cupola and a four-piece bathroom with marble shower stall and bidet. The rooms, one in pale blue and the other in pale pink, have king-size beds and modern furniture. The suite, more like a small apartment, has a wrought-iron double bed and a queen-size sleeper, and a sitting room. The rooms have radios, but no TV or phones.

The dinner menu has eight entrees, including a vegetarian dish, and there is a daily special and a daily seafood special. The wine cellar is one of the best stocked in the area, offering a number of rare vintages.

Gord has provided the recipe for one of the inn's popular entrees.

The Waterlot Sautéed Rabbit Morengo

(Serves 4)

1 rabbit, cut up
Salt and pepper to taste
3 T flour
2 T olive oil
1 T butter
1/2 cup finely chopped onion
2 T finely chopped shallots
1 t crushed garlic
1/2 cup sliced mushrooms
1 cup dry white wine
1 lb fresh tomatoes, cubed
1 t tomato paste
4 or more sprigs parsley
2 sprigs fresh thyme or 1 T crushed dry thyme
1 large bay leaf
Handful of dried prunes

Dust rabbit meat with salt and pepper and flour. Heat oil in a large frying pan over medium heat; brown rabbit. Discard fat. Add butter, onions, shallots, garlic and mushrooms; cook about 5 minutes. Stir in white wine, tomatoes and tomato paste. Bundle parsley, thyme and bay leaf in cheesecloth and add to pot. Stir in the prunes. Cover and simmer about 45 minutes. Remove rabbit pieces and herb bag. Deglaze pan and pour juices over meat when serving. (Goes well with root vegetables and mashed potatoes.)

The Oban Inn

An historic and elegant full-service country inn with fine food and pub ambience. The patio, dining room and a few of the 23 guest rooms overlook Lake Ontario.

Innkeeper:	Gary Burroughs
Address:	160 Front St., P.O. Box 94, Niagara-on-the-Lake, Ont. L0S 1J0
Telephone:	416-468-2165
Rooms:	23 rooms all with bathroom en suite
Children:	No facilities available
Pets:	Well-trained pets are welcome
Open:	Year round. Lunch 11:30–2; Afternoon tea 3–5; Dinner (two seatings in summer), 5:30–6 and 8–8:30; in winter, 6–8:30
Room rates:	$$$$
Food rates:	Lunch $; Dinner $$$
Smoking:	Smoking and no-smoking areas in dining room
Dress code:	Jacket preferred in dining room but not required
Facilities:	Piano bar
Attractions:	Shaw Festival; boutiques; boat cruise; lovely site in a beautiful historic village
Wheelchairs:	Patio, pub and dining room accessible
Directions:	On Front St. across from the golf course overlooking Lake Ontario

This is one "book" you can tell from its cover, and it's an old favorite for a long list of discerning guests. The Oban sparkles under crisp, white paint amid manicured grounds and abundant flower beds behind a white picket fence. The 1824-vintage mansion-turned-country inn appears inviting — an oasis of gracious tranquility in an increasingly popular historic village that is starting to get hectic in tourist season.

The inn is only two blocks removed from the main street, whose boutiques, patios and kitsch emporiums now draw coachloads of trippers all summer long in addition to the yachting set and Shaw Festival-goers who long considered the village their exclusive getaway preserve.

The guest rooms are all different in size, layout and furnishings. Some open on a balcony overlooking a nearby golf course and Lake Ontario, and all are furnished with antiques and decorated with fresh flower arrangements. The Oban nicely conveys the mood of a small, family-owned English country hotel whose family members quietly attend to the wants of their guests.

The lunch menu offers appetizers like potted shrimp, crustard of mushrooms, or smoked fish with King Edward VII's Sauce. There are cold entrees like Oban pork pie, fresh poached salmon, and stuffed avocado pear with seafood salad, and hot dishes like English steak and kidney pie, chicken vol au vent and quiche Lorraine.

Favorites from the list of dinner entrees are roast beef with Yorkshire pudding, rack of lamb with a garlic cream sauce and minted peach, and broiled flounder stuffed with shrimp and crab with parsley sauce. Dessert isn't an easy choice with treats like Grande Marnier frozen soufflé, carrot cake with lemon icing, English trifle and apple crisp with pouring cream.

Innkeeper Burroughs has kindly shared the recipe for King Edward VII's Sauce, one of the Oban's unique offerings. He explains: "This sauce was invented for His Royal Highness in the year 1861, long before he ascended the throne. It is meant to be served with boiled fish or meats, but also makes a good dressing for salads made with fish, game or poultry."

The Oban Inn King Edward VII's Sauce

(Makes about 2 cups)

4 salt anchovies
1/2 cup mixed chopped fresh tarragon, chervil and chives
4 hard-boiled egg yolks
1 T capers, rinsed and drained
1 t Dijon mustard
3 raw egg yolks
1 1/4 cups oil
1/3 cup tarragon vinegar

 Soak anchovies; fillet them, then rinse and dry. Blanch fresh herbs for a few seconds; drain well and press dry in a cloth. Place the hard-boiled egg yolks, anchovies, herbs, capers, mustard and raw egg yolks in a mortar and blend with the pestle. Work in the oil and the vinegar, a little at a time. Rub the sauce through a very fine sieve.

The Prince of Wales Hotel

One of Ontario's finest full-service country hotels, itself an historic site within a pretty village loaded with history and Victorian elegance.

Innkeeper:	John Wiens
Address:	6 Picton St., P.O. Box 46, Niagara-on-the-Lake, Ont. L0S 1J0
Telephone:	416-468-3246 (1-800-263-2452)
Rooms:	105 rooms and suites all with bathroom en suite
Children:	Yes
Pets:	No
Open:	Year round. Lunch noon–2:30; Dinner 6–9; Sunday brunch 11–2:30
Room rates:	$$$$$ in summer. Off-season packages available Nov.–Apr.
Food rates:	Lunch $; Dinner $$$
Smoking:	No cigars or pipes in dining rooms
Dress code:	Casual; jacket preferred in dining room at dinner
Facilities:	Three dining areas including a glassed-in patio overlooking the main street and park; the lounge overlooks gardens in Simcoe Park; indoor swimming pool, sauna, whirlpool, exercise room and platform tennis court
Attractions:	On the main street of a picture-postcard village within strolling distance of theatres, boutiques, parks; Shaw Festival

Wheelchairs: All public rooms and most guest rooms are accessible
Directions: On the main street of Niagara-on-the-Lake

It's a family affair, and therein lies the big difference between The Prince of Wales Hotel and the handful of equally elegant historic country inns in Ontario. The Wiens family doesn't just own this showplace; five members of the family work in different areas of it to ensure that all guests receive the gracious hospitality for which the inn has been renowned for decades.

The original section of the inn was built as Long's Hotel in 1864. If finding that section is important, you'll have to get one of the Wiens family to delineate it for you. The additions over the years have been so sensitively wrought that only an expert could guess — inside or out — where most of the changes were made.

One obvious exception is the greenhouse in Royals Dining Room, where the tables are under a canopy of hanging plants and behind glass walls giving a view of a pretty park with rioting flower beds and the main street.

Long's Hotel changed its name in 1901 to honor a special guest, the Prince of Wales, who shortly thereafter became Edward VII. The Wiens family acquired the 16-room property in 1975 and gradually and tastefully expanded the hotel the entire length of the block.

Guest rooms range from a smallish standard room with two queen-size beds to a two-bedroom tower suite with fireplace, full living room and kitchen area. The rooms are furnished in reproduction French provincial or traditional English furniture.

The public rooms are spacious and twinkle with polished wood and brass. There are lots of well-tended plants, and wood-burning fireplaces snap and crackle from autumn through spring. Guests may dine in Royals Dining Room — particularly popular with the local lunch crowd — and in the Queen's Royal Lounge, which is done in Victorian decor. Three Feathers Café is open from April through November.

This salmon recipe kindly provided by the Wiens family gives some idea of the innovative dishes offered on the inn's lunch and dinner menus.

The Prince of Wales Hotel Baked Atlantic Salmon on Spinach Purée Finished with Lobster Butter

(Serves 2)

4 shallots, chopped
2 oz dry white wine
2 bags fresh spinach, stems removed
1/2 lb soft butter
4 oz cooked lobster meat, chopped
2 6-oz fillets of fresh salmon with skin attached
Lemon wedges for garnish

In a saucepan, sauté shallots in a little butter. Stir in white wine and spinach; cook until leaves of spinach just become soft. Remove from heat and purée in food processor; set aside. In a bowl, mix together soft butter and chopped lobster meat; set aside.

Heat oven-proof frying pan over medium heat. Set oven to 400° F. Put salmon in pan, skin side down, and cook for two minutes. Place frying pan in oven and bake fish for 10 minutes; *do not overcook*. Remove from oven and pull skin off fish. Heat puréed spinach mixture. Stir in the lobster-butter mixture until butter is all melted into the spinach. *Do not overcook the sauce; it should be bright green*. Pour sauce onto serving plates. Place cooked salmon on sauce and garnish with lemon.

Traditions

Continental dining in an Edwardian mansion with an interesting history.

Innkeeper:	Peter Pappoulas
Address:	246 First Ave. West, North Bay, Ont. P1B 3C1
Telephone:	705-476-4600
Rooms:	No accommodation
Children:	Yes
Open:	Year round, daily. Lunch, Mon.-Fri. 11:30-3; Dinner, Mon.-Fri. 5-11; Sat. 5-midnight; Sun. 5-10. Closed Christmas Eve and Christmas Day
Food rates:	Lunch $; Dinner $$
Smoking:	No restrictions; smoke-free area available
Dress code:	Casual
Facilities:	Three fully licensed dining rooms
Attractions:	*Chief Commanda II* cruise on Lake Nipissing; Dionne Homestead Museum; North Bay Area Museum; Model Railroad Museum
Wheelchairs:	Not accessible
Directions:	From Highway 17, turn south on Cassells St., then left on First Ave. West

Peter bought this interesting house in 1983 and has established Traditions as North Bay's reliable standard of fine dining against which the cuisine of newcomers is judged. Luck isn't a factor in establishing a quality dining place, and Peter credits his 15-year stint at Holiday Inns with having taught him what dining patrons want and what brings them back again . . . and again.

On the main floor a huge double-sided fireplace with glass doors almost cuts the main dining room in half. The small dining room off to one side, and another upstairs, are ideal for private parties or business meetings.

The rooms are cozy with burgundy carpeting, quiet wall decorations and tables draped with white linen cloths and set with crystal and English china.

Things weren't always that elegant at 246 First Ave. West. After duty as the home of early settler John Ferguson, the building became a barracks for military police during the First World War. It was an apartment complex and then an office building before it became regional headquarters for the Children's Aid Society.

The lunch menu should suit every taste: five appetizers, three soups, four salads, a daily special, a dozen entrees and half a dozen sandwich combinations.

The same appetizers, soups and salads appear on the dinner menu, which expands to almost two dozen entrees, with several interesting treatments of fish and crustacean dishes.

There's a Greek rack of lamb (broiled in red wine, lemon juice and oregano), a lobster tail teamed with boneless breast of chicken in a sauce of vegetables julienne lightly sautéed in wine, Grand Marnier and cream, or fillet of pickerel pan fried in white wine, lemon juice and topped with sautéed chopped green onions and almonds.

Here's Peter's recipe for chicken cordon rouge.

Traditions Chicken Cordon Rouge
(Serves 2)

2 6-oz boneless chicken breasts	1 T butter
2 slices smoked ham	2 T maple syrup
1 oz shredded Mozzarella	1 egg, beaten
2 t finely chopped toasted almonds	Bread crumbs

Sauce

1/2 cup demiglace	2 oz maple syrup
2 oz orange juice	Finely shredded orange peel

Pound flat chicken breasts and set aside. Finely dice the ham; mix with the Mozzarella and almonds. Add salt and pepper to taste and 1 T butter; bind it all together with 2 T maple syrup. Place half the mixture in the center of each flattened chicken breast; roll up the breasts, tucking in the edges. Dip the chicken rolls in the beaten egg, then in the bread crumbs. Repeat, then place on a buttered baking dish. Bake at 325° F for 20 minutes, or until golden.

Meanwhile, mix sauce ingredients and bring to a boil. Reduce heat and simmer until reduced by 1/3. Serve over chicken.

Courtyard Restaurant

Fine French cuisine served in dining rooms on two levels of a lovely limestone building on a quiet cul de sac steeped in Ottawa history.

Innkeepers:	Phil Waserman and Gary Harper
Address:	21 George St., Byward Market, Ottawa, Ont. K1N 8W5
Telephone:	613-238-4623
Rooms:	No accommodation
Children:	Yes
Open:	Year round, daily. Lunch 11:30–2; Dinner 5:30–10; Sunday brunch 11–2. Closed Christmas and Boxing Day
Food rates:	Lunch $; Dinner $$
Smoking:	No cigars or pipes; no-smoking area available
Dress code:	Jacket preferred
Facilities:	Fully licensed dining rooms seating up to 150; outside café seating 60
Attractions:	Near Parliament Buildings; Royal Canadian Mint; Byward Market; Rideau Canal; Bytown Museum; Canadian Ski Museum; Rideau Hall
Wheelchairs:	Some dining rooms accessible
Directions:	From the Parliament Buildings go east on Wellington St. to Sussex Drive, turn left and go one block to George St.

You can feel the history all around you before you even enter the lovely limestone building at the end of a quiet cul de sac. The forerunner of today's elegant dining establishment was a log tavern built in 1827. That business venture was likely inspired by the construction of the nearby Rideau Canal, then the biggest construction project in North America.

The humble log tavern was replaced by the limestone Ottawa Hotel a decade later, and the building saw a variety of uses until it fell into disuse in 1912. Before the turn of the century Canada's last military public hanging was held in the restaurant's courtyard.

Extensive renovations in 1978 created the Courtyard Restaurant. Its cuisine and ambience ensured a dedicated following. The chef uses all market-fresh meats and vegetables for both traditional and innovative dishes, which are served on English china. Diners are surrounded by limestone walls and heavy beams.

The lunch menu offers seven appetizers and three soups; there are five salads, including chicken and orange. Daily specials are always featured, and nine entrees appeal to most palates. Choosing one of the seven desserts can be agonizing.

The dinner menu is a long read. Some of the dozen appetizers could make a handsome meal, like the Courtyard selection, a combination of smoked salmon, house pâté and baby shrimp. There's a new salad — spinach and strawberry — and then 17 entrees, some accompanied by Béarnaise, Bordelaise, peppercorn, mushroom or raspberry sauce. A marinated pork tenderloin is served with a rum and mango sauce. The house specialties are beef tenderloin Wellington, rack of lamb and a shrimp and scallop dish with tomato and basil.

Chef David Gower has made available this recipe for one of the Courtyard's popular dessert items.

Courtyard Restaurant Raspberry Cottage Cake

1 1/2 lbs day-old French bread
1 lb butter, at room temperature
2 cups sugar
6-8 cups frozen raspberries with juice, thawed
1 quart sour cream sweetened with 2 T light brown sugar
Whole fresh raspberries for garnish (optional)

Butter the inside of a 10-inch mold that is approximately 3 inches deep, and dust with sugar. Remove crusts and slice bread 1/2-inch thick. Butter one side of bread slices and line bottom and sides of the mold, pressing buttered side of bread to dish. Generously smooth additional butter over bread. Sprinkle with 1/2 cup of sugar. Add half the raspberries and juice; sprinkle with another 1/2 cup of sugar; add another layer of buttered bread. Smooth additional butter on the bread. Layer with sugar and raspberries as before. Finish with a layer of buttered and sugared bread. Cover mold with plastic wrap and place a flat plate or baking sheet on top; weigh down evenly and chill on a tray in refrigerator for 6 hours or overnight.

To serve, wrap hot damp towels around mold and invert onto a serving plate. For extra color, pour any remaining strained raspberry sauce over top and sides of cake. Serve with sweetened sour cream or creme fraiche, whipping cream or ice cream. Garnish with whole fresh raspberries, if desired.

Pelee Island Hotel

A small, friendly family-owned country hotel with home-style cooking, on a pretty and peaceful island.

Innkeepers:	Darith and Bruce Smith
Address:	West Dock, Pelee Island, Ont. N0R 1M0
Telephone:	519-724-2912
Rooms:	14 rooms all with bathroom en suite
Children:	Yes
Pets:	No
Open:	Year round, 7-1
Room rates:	$$. Off-season packages available
Food rates:	Lunch $; Dinner $$; Pub grub $
Smoking:	No restrictions; no-smoking area available
Dress code:	Casual
Facilities:	Bar/lounge, dining room overlooking West Dock and Lake Erie
Wheelchairs:	All public rooms accessible
Attractions:	All water sports including good fishing; island tours; bird display at pheasant-raising station; fall pheasant hunt; Pelee Island Heritage Centre; on bird and butterfly migration route
Directions:	In the hamlet of West Dock on Pelee Island

As you drive, bicycle or walk along the quiet roads of this peaceful island, most folks you pass will give you a friendly wave; if you're walking, it's not unusual for someone in a car or pickup truck to stop and offer you a ride. The 300 year-round residents have only themselves for company eight months of the year, so they welcome visitors. And in the summer, they get plenty of them — about 1,200 cottagers, most of whom arrive on the island by ferry from Sandusky.

There isn't a great deal to see or do on the small, flat island where one of the principal harvests now is grapes for a winery on the mainland. You can bring your car over on the ferry, a one-hour trip from either Kingsville or Leamington, or rent a bicycle to tour the island.

The rooms at Pelee Island Hotel are small, with nondescript furniture, and each has a four-piece bathroom en suite. The dining room is adjacent to the popular Bootleggers Bar and overlooks Lake Erie. The lunch menu offers a good variety of sandwiches and salads and a daily special. The dinner menu has eight entrees, all including all the trimmings from soup, salad or juice to coffee and tea.

It's home-style cooking, the servings are generous, and there's a children's menu for lunch and dinner. The following recipe from the Pelee Island Hotel's menu is one of their most popular dishes.

Pelee Island Hotel Pan Fried Pickerel
(Serves 2)

2 pickerel fillets
1 T lemon pepper
1 cup bread crumbs
1 T margarine
1/4 fresh lemon

Skin the fillets. Cut a notch at tail on both sides of the dark vein. Pull fish meat away from the dark vein. (This eliminates strong taste and small bones.) Wash fillets; pat excess water off, but leave fillets moist. Mix lemon pepper with bread crumbs; coat fillets with crumbs. In a frying pan over medium heat, melt margarine. Place fillets in pan, and cover. Cook until fillets are half cooked, then flip to other side. Squeeze lemon over fillets. Cover; continue to cook until fillets are flaky. Serve with lemon slices and tartar sauce.

Erie Beach Motor Hotel

A family owned and operated beachside hotel/motel famous in Southern Ontario for the fresh fish dinners it has been serving since 1946.

Innkeeper:	Tony Schneider
Address:	19 Walker St., Port Dover, Ont. N0A 1N0
Telephone:	519-583-1391
Rooms:	17 rooms, all with bathroom en suite
Children:	Yes
Pets:	No
Open:	Year round. Dining room: Breakfast, Mon.–Sat. 8–10, Sun. 9–10:30; Lunch, daily noon–1:30; Dinner, Mon.–Fri. 5–8, Sat. 5–8:30, Sun. 4–7. Lounge: Mon.–Thurs. 11:30–9:30, Fri.–Sat. 11:30–11, Sun. noon–7
Room rates:	$$
Food rates:	Lunch $; Dinner $$
Smoking:	No pipes or cigars in dining rooms
Dress code:	Casual
Facilities:	Three fully licensed dining rooms; meeting rooms
Attractions:	Near sandy beach on Lake Erie; Lighthouse Festival Theatre; boat cruises; fishing; Harbour Museum
Wheelchairs:	Accessible
Directions:	Facing Lake Erie in downtown Port Dover

Port Dover is believed to be home to the world's largest freshwater fishing fleet, and the kitchens of the Erie Beach hotel are only a few steps from the fleet's docking area. This explains part of the equation of the long-standing success of the Erie Beach hotel, but only part.

Other key ingredients are the ambience of the dining rooms and the friendliness of the Schneider family, at least three of whom are directly involved in the day-to-day operations. The accommodation side of the business is 17 motel-type rooms running west from the main building. The rooms are clean and basic with four-piece bathrooms en suite. They're only a couple of minutes from the public beach and a stroll from the town's main street, and reservations well in advance are required in summer.

Because of its location on a fine beach a reasonable distance from major population centers such as Hamilton, Port Dover should have turned into a welter of fast-food and kitsch outlets like some other popular Great Lakes resorts. But there's a minimum of that clutter here. Businesses along the main street are housed in buildings of stone and brick and have an air of permanence about them, probably because they enjoy a continuing volume of trade year round from the 4,000 permanent residents.

The hotel's lunch and dinner menus make few concessions to those not eager to dig into a platter of local perch or pickerel, but there are offerings of steak and shrimp, and a variety of draft beers are available by the pitcher.

Such is the following of the Erie Beach hotel cuisine that the Schneider family was able to expand into Hamilton so folks there can have their platters of crisply fried, golden brown fresh fish year round. Erie Beach Restaurant is at 77 King William St. and offers an almost identical menu as the hotel in Port Dover (tel. 416-577-1130).

With that kind of demand for fresh fish dishes, it's understandable why the Schneiders haven't offered their culinary formula for publication here. But Tony has passed along the recipe for an unusual pickle. Now you have a third use for pumpkins besides pie filling and jack o'lanterns!

André had apprenticed in Toronto, Vancouver, Ottawa, Montreal and West Palm Beach. In Toronto he was at the Windsor Arms Hotel, and he honed his expertise in Switzerland for five more years before leaving for the second time.

André's restaurant is in the two large front rooms of a former private home. André reigns in the kitchen; Kathrin works the dining rooms, seeing that unobtrusive service and a comfortable serving pace are maintained. The decor is basic and the menu is unabashedly Swiss.

How Swiss? The first eight of the 14 dinner entrees are schnitzels, the first seven named after Swiss towns and mountains. The eighth — served with asparagus and a Cheddar cheese sauce — honors Port Elgin. Even the concessions to North American palates — the chicken breast, perch and New York steak — have been given Swiss names.

The lunch menu is dominated by schnitzels but has a good mix for other tastes — perch, chicken, four salads, four soups and appetizers. Needless to say, the soup is Swiss onion! There's no nickel-and-diming here: lunch and dinner entrees are accompanied by a vegetable garnish and a choice of spaetzli, rice or roesti potatoes, a traditional Swiss potato pancake.

All the desserts are made in-house — such dishes as apple strudel, Black Forest cake, chocolate mousse and ice cream sundaes. The wine list is extensive and fairly priced, as are beer, liquor and liqueurs.

Here's André's recipe for the popular — you guessed it!

André's Veal Zurichoise

(Serves 4)

16 oz sliced veal
Salt and pepper
1 T vegetable oil
1 T butter
3 T finely chopped onions

1/2 lb fresh mushrooms, sliced
4 oz dry white wine
1 1/2 cups demiglace
4 oz 35% cream

Season veal slices with salt and pepper. Heat vegetable oil in frying pan over high heat. When oil is very hot, add seasoned veal; stir-fry 1 minute and remove from pan. Melt butter in pan; add onions and mushrooms, and sauté until slightly brown. Add the wine; reduce by half. Add demiglace and cream and simmer until sauce is the desired thickness. Just before serving, return veal to the sauce and stir to heat through. Serve immediately. (Butter noodles, rice or roesti potatoes — a traditional Swiss potato pancake — are good accompaniments to this dish.)

Kettle Creek Inn

A small, elegant, full-service country inn with fine food and a friendly pub ambience. Patio and gazebo for outdoors dining in this bustling Lake Erie resort port.

Innkeepers:	Gary and Jean Vedova
Address:	Main St., P.O. Box 2001, Port Stanley, Ont. N0L 2A0
Telephone:	519-782-3388
Rooms:	17 rooms, 3 suites with whirlpool and fireplace, 5 with bathroom en suite
Children:	Yes
Pets:	No
Open:	Year round, daily, 11-9; Sunday brunch 10-3
Room rates:	$$, including continental breakfast
Food rates:	Lunch $; Dinner $$
Smoking:	Smoking and no-smoking dining rooms
Dress code:	Country casual
Facilities:	Three dining rooms; conference room; parlor bar; gazebo for dining in English gardens

Attractions: Port Stanley Terminal Railway runs sightseeing excursions to nearby Union; *Kettle Creek Queen* operates cruises of harbor and area; near boutiques, art galleries, specialty shops
Wheelchairs: Patio, pub, gazebo and some guest rooms accessible
Directions: On Highway 4, 25 km (16 miles) south of the junction of Highways 401 and 4

Squire Samuel Price has long gone to his reward, but folks are still enjoying the summer home he built in this scenic Lake Erie port in 1849 . . . not that the Squire would recognize the place today.

In 1982 the combination of a lawyer and a school teacher (Gary's the lawyer) bought what had been for decades a 10-room summer hotel and spent a year fully restoring it. In 1990 the Vedovas increased their capacity with an addition of eight rooms, three of them suites, and full facilities for small business meetings.

The nine remaining rooms in the original building still share communal bathrooms, but the uniquely designed new rooms and suites have bathrooms en suite and some have whirlpool baths and gas fireplaces. The new rooms are furnished in pine, and the queen-size beds come out of the rooms' corners at a 45-degree angle — effective and practical.

Other nice touches include old-fashioned pedestal sinks, complimentary soaps and shampoos, terry-towel robes, coffeemaker, cable TV and fluffy duvets. All the rooms and suites overlook a landscaped courtyard.

The three dining rooms in the original inn serve daily specials and a comprehensive list of entrees — duck, lamb, fish, beef tenderloin Wellington, and perch just brought ashore by the local fishing fleet. There's prime rib of beef and Yorkshire pudding every Saturday night.

Here's one of the inn's recipes for a memorable lunch.

Kettle Creek Sauté of Shrimp and Scallops with Vegetable Confetti

(Serves 2)

1 tomato, peeled and seeded
1 carrot
1 zucchini
6 scallops
6 peeled shrimp

1 t butter
3 oz dry white wine
1 cup 35% cream
1/4 t fresh dill
Salt and pepper

Finely dice tomato, carrot and zucchini into 1/8-inch squares.

Sauté scallops and shrimp in butter until just firm, about 2–3 minutes. Remove from pan and keep warm. Add vegetables to pan; sauté until soft. Remove from pan and keep warm. Deglaze pan with the wine and add cream. Stir in dill; reduce until thick. Add a few shakes of salt and pepper. Return seafood to the pan. Pile the vegetables in a mound in the middle of a large plate. Arrange shrimp and scallops alternately around the base of the mound. Pour remaining sauce over the shellfish. Garnish with a sprig of dill.

Rossport Inn

This comfortable 1884 former railroad hotel is like a private club, but with home-style cooking and a spectacular vista of Rossport Harbour on Lake Superior.

Innkeepers:	Shelagh and Ned Basher
Address:	Bowman St., Rossport, Ont. P0T 2R0
Telephone:	807-824-3213
Rooms:	6 rooms sharing two 3-piece bathrooms
Children:	Yes
Pets:	Yes
Open:	May to Oct., daily, 7:30–11
Room rates:	$$, including full breakfast
Food rates:	Breakfast served only to guests and included in room rate. Dinner $$
Smoking:	No restrictions
Dress code:	Come as you are
Facilities:	Sauna; second-floor balcony overlooks Rossport Harbour on Lake Superior; kayaks for guests
Attractions:	Charter fishing, hiking trails, picnic areas; Rainbow Falls Provincial Park
Wheelchairs:	Dining rooms accessible; guest rooms not accessible
Directions:	On Rossport loop, 0.5 km (1/3 mile) off Trans-Canada Highway

It's down-home style accommodation with cooking to match in Ontario's version of an outport where the biggest excitement of the day is likely to be the evening return of the sport fishermen with their day's catch. Rossport and its inn epitomize getting away from the hassles of business and city life.

It's the sort of place that inspires the most lethargic to stroll the quiet village streets overlooking the harbor before returning to fireside — if it's a damp day — or the sun deck if it's bright and warm. Within minutes of checking in, you can become a member of the household and the community, if you wish, because these are friendly folk who welcome new faces.

The dining rooms are larger versions of what you'd find in the home of a country relative. There are antiques galore on the refinished hardwood floors and bookcases crammed with books. They overflow the cases and spread around the homey inn, onto shelves in every guest room.

The guest rooms are small, clean and cozy and decorated with old prints and antique dressers. Five of the rooms each have one double bed and the sixth has a double and a single; all are covered in Hudson's Bay blankets in case the evenings turn chilly.

The dinner menu, with 14 entrees, has something for everyone, including five dishes of local fish. The steaks weigh 13 ounces and the Cuban lobster tails weigh 13 ounces. All dinners include a relish tray, soup or salad, home-baked bread, choice of potato or rice and fresh vegetable.

This is not the sort of restaurant where anyone counts the cups of coffee, or where guests leave the table hungry. Dessert favorites are the house cheesecake and blueberry pie baked with berries picked just down the road.

The inn is used as a base by sport fishermen, and one of the menu's most popular dishes is Trout Hemingway, named, as Ned explains, "for that well-known fisherman and writer."

Rossport Inn's Trout Hemingway

(Serves 2)

4 wedges of lemon
2 fresh trout fillets
1/2 cup toasted sesame seeds
2 t flour (approx)
2 t butter
2 t dried minced onion
2 t dried basil
1/4 t paprika
Parsley for garnish

Squeeze the juice of lemon wedges over one side of skinless trout fillets. Sprinkle with toasted sesame seeds. Sprinkle with flour from a shaker. Heat butter in frying pan and sauté the fillets, sesame-seeded side down. Cook until the edges of the fillets turn white and the sesame seeds turn brown, approximately 4 minutes. Invert the fillets into a glass baking dish. Sprinkle with dried minced onion, basil and paprika. Dot with butter. Cover with a paper towel. Pour over the towel enough water to just cover the bottom of the dish. Microwave on High for about 4 minutes, or until fish flakes. Garnish with parsley and serve.

The Brickyard Restaurant and Bar

A popular restaurant in a turn-of-the-century stable. There are inventive and enticing lunch, dinner and pub-grub menus and a separate area for dancing.

Innkeeper:	Al Levy
Address:	708 Queen St. East, Sault Ste. Marie, Ont. P6A 2A9
Telephone:	705-759-2201
Rooms:	No accommodation
Children:	Yes
Open:	Year round, Mon.–Sat. noon–1 a.m.
Food rates:	Lunch $; Dinner $$; Pub food $
Smoking:	No restrictions
Dress code:	Casual
Facilities:	Dining room and lounge; live music for dancing nightly
Attractions:	Agawa Canyon rail excursion; Soo Locks tours; Charles Ermatinger Stone House; Art Gallery; M.S. *Norgama* Museum; Sault Ste. Marie Museum; Fort St. Joseph National Historic Site; St. Joseph Island Museum
Wheelchairs:	Lounge and dining room accessible
Directions:	In downtown Sault Ste. Marie, corner of Queen and East streets

The Brickyard has many faces. It's a modern concept inside walls that are ancient by Soo standards — which is how the natives refer to Sault Ste. Marie. It's a great place to meet people and it's a rendezvous for the young movers in town.

It's the sort of place where you'd expect management to have found a few popular dishes and stuck with them. That concept would normally fit with the scrap art on the otherwise bare stone and brick walls, the bare hardwood floors and the jungles of hanging plants.

The first surprise is that the menu isn't limited to nachos, chicken wings and ribs. The next surprise is that the menu changes daily while a number of house specialties remain. And the best surprise is the menus themselves; they offer tastes of Greece and Italy, the Far East, the Deep South and a variety of places in between. Here's an item off the lunch menu: Sherried Crab, a lightly seasoned creamy mixture with mushrooms, green onions and fresh chopped tomatoes, served open-faced on a butterflied butter croissant.

You could find similar dishes on the lunch and dinner menus in most good restaurants, but at The Brickyard almost all of them have extra touches to excite the taste buds.

The Brickyard has offered the recipe for this popular dish from their menu.

The Brickyard Basil Chicken

(Serves 2)

2 4-oz boneless, skinless chicken breasts, cut in strips

Freshly ground black pepper

4 T fresh chopped basil (or 2 T dry)

1 T fresh minced garlic

3 oz olive oil

10 oz mushrooms, sliced

8 sun-dried tomatoes (stored in oil), cut in thin strips

8 strips green pepper

4 slices fresh tomato

4 green onions, chopped

4-6 T pine nuts

Grated Parmesan cheese for garnish

Season chicken with pepper, basil and garlic. In a deep frying pan, sauté chicken in olive oil until chicken begins to brown, but do not brown garlic. Add mushrooms, sun-dried tomatoes, green pepper, tomato slices, onions and pine nuts, tossing after each addition. When chicken is cooked and vegetables are heated through, serve on cooked spinach noodles or other pasta. Garnish with Parmesan cheese.

Cesira's Italian Cuisine

Cesira is the chef. The recipes backing up the menu for five dining rooms in two connected turn-of-the-century houses were handed down by her mother.

Innkeeper:	Frank Aiudi
Address:	133-137 Spring St., Sault Ste. Marie, Ont. P6A 3A2
Telephone:	705-949-0600
Rooms:	No accommodation
Children:	Yes
Open:	Year round, daily, 11–11; Sat. and Sun. 5–11. Closed holidays
Food rates:	Lunch $; Dinner $$
Smoking:	No pipes or cigars
Dress code:	Casual
Facilities:	Four small dining rooms accommodating 14 persons each; one holding 22 persons
Attractions:	Agawa Canyon rail excursion; Soo Locks tours; Charles Ermatinger Stone House; Art Gallery; M.S. *Norgama* Museum; Sault Ste. Marie Museum; Fort St. Joseph National Historic Site; St. Joseph Island Museum
Wheelchairs:	Not accessible
Directions:	Just off Queen St. in downtown Sault Ste. Marie

This is one restaurant that's properly named, so don't go looking for roast beef and Yorkshire pudding or barbecued ribs on the menu. There are some steaks — poivre, Diane, tartare, New York, filet mignon, sirloin and Chateaubriand — but it's the traditional Italian food that keeps the regulars coming back for heaped, steaming plates of Cesira's family dishes.

The pasta is made in Cesira's kitchen and used in such dishes as fettuccini, lasagna, ravioli, cannelloni and tortellini. Other Italian dishes feature giant tiger shrimp, Lake Superior lake trout, lobster tail, king crab and veal.

There is roast beef, but forget the Yorkshire. This beef is pasticciata — roast beef Italian-style. And there are French dishes like shrimp flamed in Pernod and lobster tails flamed in brandy at your table.

The lunch menu makes a number of concessions to North America — a good sandwich selection, homemade pie, salads and steaks — but the popular home-style Italian dishes predominate.

The small dining rooms are intimate and subtly lighted and were formed when two houses on Spring Street were ingeniously joined under one roof in 1977. There is, of course, a good wine list. Cesira has offered one of her family recipes — not particularly recommended for those trying to maintain svelte waistlines!

Cesira's Fettuccini Alfredo

(Serves 2 or makes 4 appetizers)

12 oz fettuccini	2 T butter
1 1/4-1 1/2 cups 35% cream	2 T grated Parmesan or Romano cheese

Cook fettuccini in salted boiling water until almost at desired consistency. Meanwhile, in a separate saucepan warm the cream and butter over medium-high heat. Strain fettuccini and add to saucepan, stirring constantly for about 2 minutes, or until sauce thickens. Remove from heat and mix in grated cheese.

Severn River Inn

An historic country inn with 10 rooms and reasonably priced fine dining, on the banks of the Severn River at the southern entrance to Muskoka.

Innkeepers:	Louise Fox and Don Moreton
Address:	Cowbell Lane, Box 100, Severn Bridge, Ont. P0E 1N0
Telephone:	705-689-6333
Rooms:	10 rooms with bathroom en suite
Children:	Yes
Pets:	No
Open:	Year round. May–Thanksgiving, daily except Tuesdays; Thanksgiving–Dec., Wed.–Sun.; Jan. through Apr., Thurs.–Sun. Lunch noon–closing; Afternoon tea 2:30–5; Dinner 5:30–9; Bar open to 11 p.m.; Sunday brunch 11–2:30. Open Christmas and New Year's Day
Room rates:	$$, including full breakfast. Lower rates in winter
Food rates:	Lunch $; Dinner $$
Smoking:	No restrictions; smoke-free area available
Dress code:	Informal
Facilities:	Fully licensed dining room; screened verandah and patio overlooking the river; fully licensed restaurant

Attractions:	Near Stephen Leacock Home in Orillia; Dr. Norman Bethune Home in Gravenhurst; R.M.S. *Segwun* cruises; Santa's Village; near studios of local artists and artisans
Wheelchairs:	Restaurant and dining room accessible; not all guest rooms accessible
Directions:	Just off Highway 11 at Cowbell Lane, immediately north of the bridge over the Severn River

Its legitimate history gives this inn one of two magnets to draw visitors from hectic Highway 11, which passes almost too close to its doors. (The other magnet is the dining.) The building was designed as a country store that contained the post office and telephone exchange, and there were rooms for teachers, travelers and summer guests.

That was back in 1907, and the exterior hasn't been tampered with since. Today a sign informs that the building is an inn, but guests enter what looks like an old Muskoka general store. The former store now contains tables and chairs and a small bar, and meals are served from breakfast through supper to late-night snacks. General store artifacts and collectibles hang from the rafters and walls.

The dining room is at the "back" of the building, which fronts on a placid stretch of the Severn River and has a more formal atmosphere. A pillared and screened verandah where lunch and dinner are served is off the dining room overlooking the lawns and the river. A small dining area, designated The Parlor, is often used for private parties and intimate dinners. It has a large bay window with a view of the river.

Upstairs are cozy guest rooms. The furniture is turn-of-the-century Victoriana. There are lace cushions and eyelet bedspreads on the beds and antique samplers and needlepoints on the walls.

The restaurant in the former general store is called The Store Front and its menu defies simple description, unless perhaps it's a lesson in geography. You could start with French onion soup and then have an Italian or Greek salad. Entrees include Swiss burger, souvlaki, quiche, Mexican pie, steak and mushroom pie and tortière. (There are many other choices; I've listed just those whose nationality was obvious.)

The Dining Room's dinner menu is a bit more traditional but still features dishes from a range of distant places. The vegetables and herbs and spices come from the inn's garden in season.

Louise, who used to own a catering business in Toronto, has developed many of the desserts, all of which are made in-house along with the baked goods.

Both menus have something for every palate, and the prices in both dining spots are pleasingly low. The summer and tourist traffic would easily support higher prices, but Don and Louise have been carefully building a year-round local trade since they bought the property in 1987.

Here's Louise's torta recipe.

Severn River Torta Rustica

Whole wheat pastry (recipe follows)
2 1/2 lb spinach
3 cloves garlic, minced
3 T butter
6 eggs

1 cup grated Parmesan cheese
3 cups ricotta cheese
8 T chopped fresh basil (or 3 T dried)
1 lb thinly sliced cooked ham
3 cups grated Mozzarella cheese

Preheat oven to 400° F.

Roll out the pastry to approximately 1/4-inch thick and line the bottom and sides of a 10-inch springform pan, leaving the dough overhanging the sides of the pan.

Blanch the spinach, drain well and chop coarsely. Sauté the spinach in the garlic and butter until all the moisture has evaporated. Set aside. Beat the eggs; stir in the Parmesan, ricotta and basil. Fill the pastry crust, beginning with one third of the sliced ham, followed by half of the Mozzarella cheese, half of the spinach and half of the egg-cheese mixture. Repeat the layers once and top with the remaining ham. Fold the pastry from the sides over the top. The pastry will not quite meet, but this allows the steam to escape during cooking.

Bake the torta for 60 minutes or until the pastry is slightly browned and a knife inserted comes out clean. Remove the torta from the oven and leave in the pan for at least 15 minutes to cool and set. Release the springform and invert the torta. Serve hot or cold, cut into wedges.

Whole Wheat Pastry
4 cups whole wheat flour
4 T brown sugar

1 1/2 cups cold butter, cut in 1/4-inch pieces
2/3 cup cold water

Place the flour and sugar in a food processor, add the chopped butter and water, and process until the mixture begins to clump. The dough will be soft. Place the dough in a plastic bag and refrigerate for half an hour before rolling out.

Mrs. Mitchell's

Fine traditional country dining in an 1889 one-room school house enlarged to two rooms each with an open-face wood-burning fireplace.

Innkeepers:	Jim and Maureen Baufeldt
Address:	R.R. 4, Shelburne, Ont. L0N 1X8
Telephone:	519-925-3627
Rooms:	No accommodation
Children:	Yes
Open:	Year round, Tues.–Sun. and holiday Mondays. Lunch, Tues.–Fri. 12–2; Sat. & Sun. brunch 11–2; Dinner, Tues.–Sun. 5–9:30; Afternoon tea 2–4
Food rates:	Lunch $; Dinner $$
Smoking:	No pipes or cigars
Dress code:	Country casual
Facilities:	Fully licensed; two dining rooms; two open-face wood-burning fireplaces; antique decorations; gift shop; manicured grounds shaded by mature trees
Attractions:	Near Collingwood's Blue Mountain ski facility and Great Slide Ride; Collingwood Museum; Bruce Trail; Mansfield Skiways; Base Borden Military Museum near Barrie; Centennial Beach Park

Wheelchairs: Accessible
Directions: In Violet Hill on Highway 89 between Highway 10 and Airport Rd.

Mrs. Mitchell ran Mulmur Township School Section 2 until it fell victim to the central school scheme in 1968. In recognition of her two decades of dedication to area youngsters, Jim and Maureen named their restaurant after her.

It's a cozy, comfortable place with large bay windows that fit in nicely with the historic ambience, lots of greenery and a wealth of pewter, brass and copper artifacts. The walls are decorated with seventeenth-century stencils, and as you enter, you'll notice the outline of pineapples stenciled on the floor, a symbol of welcome in seventeenth-century England.

On chilly days, flames flicker in the fireplaces and their reflections twinkle off polished woodwork and give new depths to the oil paintings displayed on the walls.

Nearby is a gift shop with clothing, Canadian handcrafts and books on cooking, gardening, travel and history.

The lunch menu is short but tempting: Mrs. Mitchell's Brunswick Stew, for example, is made from young fowl and vegetables and served with a garden salad; country beef stew in a red wine sauce is also served with a salad.

There's a Cheddar and crabmeat omelette, country sausages with spiced apples, chicken breast on rice with Hibernian sauce or baked French onion soup with crusty roll and pot of Cheddar. Hot drop biscuits and sweet potato muffins accompany the entrees.

For appetizers there's a daily soup, clam chowder, salad and mulled apple cider. Desserts include hot Dutch apple pie, raspberry cream pie, rum cream pie and trifle.

Pâté laced with sherry joins the appetizer list on the dinner menu, and there are eight entrees: two beef dishes, pork, duckling, chicken, rack of lamb and two fish. The duckling comes under an orange sauce; the pork loin is stuffed and has spiced apples on the side, and the lamb is with a Madeira sauce. The chicken is stuffed with crabmeat, the tenderloin of beef has a brandy cream sauce, and the prime ribs are au jus with horseradish.

All entrees are accompanied by a crusty roll, salad, vegetables and spoon bread, and Maureen has shared the spoon bread recipe. She says the recipe "just happened" when a corn bread batter was left too long in a hot oven.

Mrs. Mitchell's Spoon Bread

(Serves 8)

1 1/2 cups water
2 cups milk
1 1/2 cups cornmeal
1 1/4 t salt

1 1/2 t sugar
2 T butter
5 eggs
1 T baking powder

Preheat oven to 350° F. Grease a large, shallow baking dish. In a saucepan, combine the water and milk and heat to simmer. Add the cornmeal, salt, sugar and butter, and stir over medium heat until the mixture is thickened, about 5 minutes. Remove from heat. Beat the eggs with the baking powder until they are light and fluffy. Mix into the cornmeal mixture. Pour batter into the prepared baking dish and bake for 45–50 minutes. Serve hot.

Benjamin's Restaurant and Inn

A re-created 1852 country inn with antiques in the guest rooms and an open-hearth fireplace in a licensed dining room serving country and contemporary cuisine.

Innkeepers:	Sandy Shantz
Address:	17 King St., St. Jacobs, Ont. N0B 2N0
Telephone:	519-664-3731
Rooms:	9 rooms with bathroom en suite
Children:	Yes
Pets:	No
Open:	Sun.–Thurs. 11:30–9; Fri. & Sat. 11:30–10
Room rates:	$$$$, including continental breakfast. Special midweek package Jan.–Apr.
Food rates:	Lunch $; Dinner $$
Smoking:	No cigars or pipes in dining room
Dress code:	Casual
Facilities:	Seminar room for up to 14 people; continental breakfast for guests on windowed verandah; outdoor patio
Attractions:	Next door to and across the street from more than 40 artisan and craft shops and boutiques; Maple Syrup Museum of Ontario; The Meeting Place

Wheelchairs: Dining room accessible
Directions: In downtown St. Jacobs

It's a lot fancier than when Joseph Eby opened it as Farmers' Inn back in 1852. Then it was a stage-coach stop for passengers who were traveling to get somewhere — instead of away from somewhere. Most of today's guests at Benjamin's go there to stay because they want to, not because it's the only place to rest on their journey.

Some rooms are furnished in reproduction Canadian antiques and are bright, roomy and restfully decorated. Other rooms contain traditional furniture. All rooms have TV and a clock radio and some have handmade Mennonite quilts on the beds.

At lunch there's a daily quiche, pasta plate and fish dish, a short list of appetizers and four salads. The dinner menu offers eight appetizers and eight entrees appealing to just about every taste — there's fish, chicken, lamb, pork, pasta, veal and beefsteak.

The dining-room tables are of cherry wood, the ceiling beams are pine and there's lots of greenery from potted and hanging plants. The decor features antiques and hand-painted pottery, and fresh cut flowers adorn each table. In cold weather a fire crackles in the open-hearth fireplace. The cuisine is mainly French, but there are some traditional Mennonite dishes. The following recipe is for one of the more popular items on Benjamin's menu.

Benjamin's Sweet Potato and Green Onion Pancakes with Goat Cheese and Sun-dried Tomato Cream

(Serves 2–4)

4 medium sweet potatoes	1 t butter
2 green onions, roughly chopped	1 shallot, finely sliced
1 egg	2 T white wine (optional)
Pinch of salt	2/3 cup whipping cream
Pinch of pepper	3 sun-dried tomatoes, cut in thin strips
2 t olive oil	1–2 oz goat cheese, crumbled

Roast sweet potatoes in 425° F oven for 40–50 minutes until slightly undercooked. Let cool. Peel. Grate cooled potatoes into a small mixing bowl. Add green onions, egg, salt and pepper; mix together. Form mix into 4-inch rounds 3/8-inch thick and set on waxed paper.

Put a large, non-stick frying pan on high heat. When pan is hot, add olive oil and quickly add butter. Reduce heat to medium. Sauté pancakes until nicely brown on both sides.

In a separate small pan, heat shallots and white wine together; let reduce by 3/4. Add cream and sun-dried tomatoes; reduce until slightly thick. Add goat cheese and season with salt and pepper. Arrange pancakes on plate and pour sauce over. Serve immediately.

The Unicorn Inn and Restaurant

Exceptional dining from an imaginative menu in a converted 1904 pioneer homestead in a secluded valley on 440 acres of untrammeled rural beauty.

Innkeepers:	David and Arlan Nobel
Address:	R.R. 1, South Gillies, Thunder Bay, Ont. P0T 2V0
Telephone:	807-475-4200
Rooms:	3 guest rooms sharing a 4-piece and a 2-piece bathroom; 1 light housekeeping cottage
Children:	Yes for B & B, over 10 for dining; babysitting available by arrangement
Pets:	No
Open:	Feb.–Dec. Dinner: Thurs.–Sat. 7 p.m.; Sun. 5 p.m. All seatings by reservation only. Closed Halloween, Christmas Eve and Christmas Day
Room rates:	$$. Cottage $$$$. Includes full breakfast
Food rates:	Dinner $$$–$$$$
Smoking:	No smoking in the inn or cottage
Dress code:	None
Facilities:	Two fully licensed dining rooms seating 40 diners; living room for guests
Attractions:	Near Old Fort William; Kakabeka Falls; Mt. McKay; International Friendship Gardens; cruise ship *Welcome*; amethyst mines
Wheelchairs:	Several steps to dining room; washroom accessible
Directions:	From Thunder Bay, drive south on Highway 61 for 20 km (12 1/2 miles) from the Thunder Bay Airport. Turn right onto Highway 608 at the sign for South Gillies. Follow Highway 608 for 16 km (11 miles). At the bottom of the hill turn right onto Unicorn Rd. Unicorn Road ends at the inn.

The cuisine awaiting the visitor to Ontario's most remote country inn far outweighs the daunting logistics of getting there. And for the overnight guest, the quiet of those wide open spaces is additional repayment. (Perhaps the Unicorn isn't Ontario's most remote country inn — but it is certainly the most remote country inn listed in this book.)

Arlan and David are transplanted Americans who have brought the ambience of a European pension to the province's north woods. And they've done it with a culinary flair and expertise embraced by gourmands beyond their wildest hopes.

After two and a half years of renovating their wilderness settler's home as a bed and breakfast operation with room for up to 14 dinner guests, the Nobels held their grand opening in 1984.

Word of the extraordinarily excellent cuisine spread rapidly. Would-be dinner guests, told The Unicorn was fully booked, pleaded to be allowed to dine standing in the kitchen! So dining tables spread out into the living room to accommodate up to 40. Despite this, there still are lots of disappointed folks who can't get a reservation the night they want it.

Only complete seven-course dinners are served, and although the menu lists 17 entrees, only one entree is served each evening. That dish is chosen by the first party to reserve for that particular evening. There are six seafood entrees, four of chicken and turkey, three of "sophisticated fowl," an Italian dinner, and lamb, veal tenderloin and filet of beef specialties.

The "sophisticated fowl" dishes have developed a considerable following. David uses pintelles, young, French-bred guinea fowls, and a port and cognac cream sauce or a Marsala wine and butter reduction sauce.

The guest rooms are small but bright and simply appointed. Beds, desks and armoires are of knotty pine, and each room has at least one framed unicorn print on the lemon-colored walls. The cottage is a great getaway retreat; its bay windows overlook the empty reaches of the valley.

Typical of the lengths to which he will go to create something unusual to titillate a guest's taste buds is this recipe David has kindly shared.

The Unicorn's Cactus Pear Sherbet

(Makes 1 1/2–2 quarts)

1 1/2–2 limes
5 lbs cactus pears
6–8 oranges, preferably Valencia

1 1/2 cups sugar
3–4 t dark rum
1 1/2 cups sugar

Juice the limes; strain and set aside. *Wearing rubber gloves* as protection from the prickles, peel the cactus pears. Push the flesh through a medium sieve to extract as much juice and pulp as possible (5 lbs pears should yield 4 cups). Juice the oranges; strain the juice, pushing as much pulp through the sieve as possible. Measure out 2 cups. Heat 1 1/2 cups of orange juice with the sugar over low heat until the sugar is just dissolved. Add to remaining 1/2 cup of orange juice. Stir in the pear juice. Stir in lime juice and rum to taste. Chill. Place in ice cream maker and freeze according to manufacturer's instructions.

Serve in combination with passion fruit, pineapple, lemon or tropical fruit sherberts and/or coconut or vanilla ice cream.

Chantry House Inn

A small country inn with suites fashioned from an 1880 home. The imaginative lunch and dinner menus feature Mennonite recipes handed down through the hosts' families.

Innkeepers:	David and Diane Snyder
Address:	118 High St., Southampton, Ont. N0H 2L0
Telephone:	519-797-2646
Rooms:	5 suites all with bathroom en suite. Rooms available by reservation only
Children:	Well-behaved children over 10 are accepted
Pets:	No. A kennel is nearby
Open:	Year round, daily, noon–9 p.m. Sunday brunch Victoria Day–Thanksgiving, 11–2. Open Christmas Day by reservation only
Room rates:	$$$, including continental breakfast. Special packages available year round
Food rates:	Lunch $; Dinner $$. Meals by reservation only
Smoking:	Dining rooms designated smoking and no-smoking. No smoking in four of the five suites. A smoking area is available in the inn
Dress code:	Jacket preferred in dining room
Facilities:	Beer and wine license for dining rooms; gift shop of handcrafts; dinner guests are entertained by the host on a Steinway Reproducing Grand Piano on designated dinner concert evenings

Attractions:	Near sandy beach on Lake Huron with mile-long boardwalk; Bruce County Museum; Bruce Nuclear Power Development; MacGregor Point Provincial Park; Chantry Island lighthouse
Wheelchairs:	Not accessible
Directions:	On the north side of High St., midway between Southampton's main street and the beach

Guests entering this delightful inn must sometimes wonder whether they've mistakenly walked into a private home. That's the ambience of the place and the feeling innkeepers David and Diane Snyder want to create. They are dedicated to *freundschaft* — German for friendship — and they've amassed an impressive roster of repeat guests because that's also their business philosophy.

Seven generations ago, David's ancestor Joseph Schneider was a founder of Kitchener who gained a wide reputation for his fine meats and cheeses. The name remains on the products of that well-known packing house, but Joseph's descendants Americanized their name early in this century.

Suites in the inn and an annex are decorated with family heirlooms and antiques. The rooms have ceiling fans and the dining rooms and all guest suites are air-conditioned. Each suite is a different size and configuration, but all have couches stuffed with feathers.

All guest accommodations have coffeemakers, mini-refrigerators and microwave ovens; there are guest common rooms on each floor and a boardroom for small meetings. Diane made all the afghans on the beds and the sheets and curtains, and her talented decorating touches are evident throughout the property.

There are no telephones in the suites (unless guests request one) because this is a haven for those who want to get away from outside pressures. Although there are color TVs in the suites, their screens are small. "That's to remind guests to keep the volume low so they won't disturb a neighbor," David explains.

The lunch and dinner menus change frequently, and in summer, vegetables are from the Snyders' garden. All dishes are prepared from scratch in the kitchen, and the jams, jellies and preserves are all made on the premises. Meals are served on Wedgwood, Limoges or Spode china.

Diane has shared the recipe for one of her most popular dishes.

Chantry House Inn Cream Puffs, Mennonite Style

(Makes 6 cream puffs)

2/3 cup water
1/3 cup butter
2/3 cup all purpose flour
1/4 t salt
3 large eggs

Preheat oven to 450° F. Combine water and butter in a heavy saucepan and bring to a rapid boil. Reduce heat to medium. Add flour and salt. Using a wooden spoon, stir vigorously until mixture forms a ball. Cool 5 minutes. Add eggs one at a time, beating well with a wooden spoon. Divide into six round mounds on an ungreased baking sheet. Place in oven and lower the heat to 400° F; bake for 40 minutes. Cool on a rack. When cool, slice off top of each cream puff, pick out centers and use in one of the following ways.

Fill with ice cream, fresh fruits, puddings or whipped creams. Try a little chocolate sauce, jam or maple syrup on top after filling. Diane says she likes to experiment with cream puffs by varying the shapes, sizes and fillings. She says tiny cream puffs make wonderful appetizers when filled with cocktail fillings; large ones are great for lunch or dinner when filled with hot creamed chicken, mushrooms or seafood.

Rockgarden Terrace Resort

A small, family owned and operated year-round resort offering all outdoor sports, health spa and fine Canadian and continental cuisine with an Austrian flavor.

Innkeepers:	The Oswald Argmann family
Address:	R.R. 1, Spring Bay, Ont. P0P 2B0
Telephone:	705-377-4652
Rooms:	18 modern motel units on three levels; 4 Swiss chalet-style cabins; 1 fully equipped two-bedroom cottage with fireplace and deck
Children:	Yes
Pets:	No
Open:	Year round. Breakfast 7–10; Lunch 11:30–2; Dinner 5–9
Room rates:	$$$. Off-season packages available
Food rates:	Lunch $; Dinner $$
Smoking:	No pipes or cigars in dining room; smoking in designated areas
Dress code:	Casual
Facilities:	On Lake Mindemoya; swimming pool, whirlpool, sauna, health spa, shuffleboard, putting green, outdoor chess, nature trails, cross-country skiing, golf nearby

Attractions:	Rockgarden Terrace Resort is in the middle of the 1,055-square-mile Manitoulin Island — the largest freshwater island in the world — which attracts hunters, fishermen, artists, photographers and yachtsmen. The island is rugged but scenic, and there are interesting museums and sights in the small communities
Wheelchairs:	Not accessible
Directions:	From Highway 6 at Little Current, take secondary highway 540 to West Bay, then Highway 551 to Crosshill Road and follow the signs. From South Baymouth, take Highway 6 to secondary highway 542 through Mindemoya to the fifth sideroad and follow signs.

The resort property is perched atop a limestone cliff overlooking Lake Mindemoya. For guests who don't favor the hike down to the lake, a heated outdoor swimming pool also overlooks the lake. So do the dining room, the health spa, the chalets and all of the 18 modern motel units on three levels. The motel units are large, well designed and have four-piece bathrooms en suite. The furniture is contemporary. A wide verandah on each level overlooks the lake.

The property has been developed since 1974 by the Argmann family and is very much a family affair. Mother Angela applies her expertise in the kitchen, Father Oswald manages the operation and jollies the guests, and daughters Ossie, Heidi and Carmen all pitch in as well.

Guests can remain aloof from that environment or get involved in it and become a part of the friendly family for the duration of their stay.

The resort invites lazy days with a book beside the pool or on a motel unit verandah, or you can be up at dawn chasing pickerel, whitefish and perch in the lake, or salmon and trout in spring and fall in the Mindemoya River. In winter, cross-country ski trails and snowmobile trails start at the front door.

The resort property even contains one of Manitoulin's tourist attractions. In the cliff on which the resort stands, there's a limestone cave discovered in 1888 by three Mennonite preachers who were hunting. Inside the cave they found the skeletons of seven Indians, believed to have been Ottawa Indians hiding from Iroquois who overran the island in 1652. (The skeletons were removed to a Toronto museum, which was subsequently destroyed by fire.) The cave is lighted and contains some interesting displays.

The dining room's menu offers a dozen entrees, three of them different treatments of veal cutlets. There are also chicken and fish dishes, Hungarian goulash, shrimp and several steaks. Angela has kindly shared the recipe for the house specialty.

Rockgarden Terrace Viennese Veal Cutlets

(Serves 6)

2 lbs veal cutlets
2 T flour
6 T dry bread crumbs
1 t salt
1/4 t black pepper
4 T butter
1 egg, beaten
6 thin slices lemon

Cut veal into 6 serving-size pieces. Mix together flour, bread crumbs, salt and pepper. Melt butter in a heavy frying pan over medium heat. Dip veal in beaten egg, then in flour mixture. Brown on both sides in butter, adding butter if needed. Transfer veal to a hot platter and top each cutlet with a lemon slice.

The Chequers

The dishes of rural France and Spain are served with traditional European flair in an historic three-story, Gothic-style 1868 country tavern.

Innkeepers:	Denise and Jose-Luis Perez
Address:	5816 Hazeldean Rd., Stittsville, Ont. K2S 1B9
Telephone:	613-836-1665
Rooms:	No accommodation
Children:	Yes
Open:	Year round. Lunch, Mon.–Fri. 11:30–2:30; Dinner, Mon.–Sat. 5:30–10:30. Closed Sundays, Christmas and New Year's Day
Food rates:	Lunch $$; Dinner $$$
Smoking:	No restrictions; smoke-free area available
Dress code:	Informal
Facilities:	Three fully licensed dining rooms; small cocktail bar on ground floor; bar-lounge with tapas on second floor
Attractions:	About 25 km (15 miles) southwest of all the attractions of Ottawa
Wheelchairs:	Ground floor bar and dining rooms accessible
Directions:	Off the Queensway west of Ottawa, exit Terry Fox Dr., continue south to Hazeldean Rd. (old Highway 7)

The historic building is ideally suited to it, but the visitor wandering eastern Ontario is still not prepared for a fine restaurant with a very English name, owned and operated by a delightful Spanish-English couple and offering the dishes of France and Spain.

It all makes sense when owner Jose-Luis explains the background in accented English that recalls wonderful sojourns in numerous resorts along Spain's Mediterranean coast. (Jose-Luis is from Spain's Atlantic coast, but the accent and gestures are the same.) He trained in France and then polished his culinary skills for nine years in England at a place called The Chequers. He and Denise bought the historic Kemp's Tavern in 1982 and began treating guests to the delights of Spanish and French country cooking.

For unadventurous palates the lunch and dinner menus offer standard continental fare: pâté, smoked salmon, sirloin steak, roast duckling, fresh fish and broiled lamb. But for those who would banish a chill Canadian evening by tucking into dishes from old Espana and fondly recalling that sun-soaked country, there are dishes like gazpacho Andaluz, shrimps in garlic Madrid-style, rabbit casserole la riojana and partridge old-country-style.

The dining rooms help get you in the mood, too. There are dark, moody paintings of Spanish scenes, lots of stained glass windows, and the tables are covered with crisp, white linen set with crystal and spotless silverware. Table service is performed with deft panache.

Jose-Luis's apprenticeship in France shows up on the menus as well: escargots de bourgogne, mussels and shrimp provençale, suprême of pheasant with peaches and brandy and suprême of chicken à l'orange. (The escalopes of Buffalo "chasseur" just sneaked into the kitchen and got a French name!)

Executive chef Kenneth Paterson has made the recipe for the following popular dish available.

The Chequers Seafood Costa Brava
(Serves 4)

8 oz white wine	8 scallops
20 oz fish stock	Pinch of saffron
2 lobster tails, cut in half lengthwise	2 oz tomato sauce
10 oz monkfish fillets, sliced into medallions	2 oz garlic butter, softened
12 mussels, cleaned	Salt and pepper to taste
8 shrimp, peeled and deveined	4 oz snipped chives for garnish

In a large saucepan, bring wine and stock to the boil and reduce by 1/3. In the following order at one-minute intervals add: the lobster tails, monkfish, mussels, shrimp and scallops. Simmer until everything is cooked — about 1 minute after adding the scallops. Using a slotted spoon, transfer seafood to a serving dish and keep warm. Stir saffron and tomato sauce into cooking liquid; reduce by 1/3. Remove from heat. Whisk in soft garlic butter. Add salt and pepper. Pour hot sauce over seafood in serving dish and sprinkle with snipped chives. Serve immediately.

Queen's Inn at Stratford

A Stratford landmark fully restored to its 1853 elegance. In the public rooms, visitors can enjoy French cuisine, Victorian decor or a popular brew pub.

Innkeepers:	Crozier and Tim Taylor
Address:	161 Ontario St., Stratford, Ont. N5A 3H3
Telephone:	519-271-1400
Rooms:	31 rooms and suites all with bathroom en suite
Children:	Yes
Pets:	No
Open:	Year round. Brew pub 11:30–1 a.m.; Dining room 5–9; Piano lounge 8 a.m.–1 a.m.; Sunday brunch 11:30–2
Room rates:	$$$, including continental breakfast. Off-season packages available
Food rates:	Lunch $; Dinner $$; Pub grub $
Smoking:	No restrictions
Dress code:	No jeans
Facilities:	Four distinctly different dining areas including a brew pub with its own brand of draft beer
Attractions:	The Stratford Festival; changing art exhibits in The Gallery; beautiful parks along the Avon River

Wheelchairs: All public rooms accessible and 1 guest room is specially fitted to accommodate the handicapped
Directions: In downtown Stratford, corner of Ontario and Waterloo streets

Stratford's oldest existing hotel was given a new lease on life in 1988 and offers guests all modern comforts within its walls, which were erected in 1853. A complete renovation and refurbishment by Crozier Taylor and his son Tim transformed a seedy dowager on a downtown corner to the Grand Old Lady of the Stratford hospitality sector.

The Taylor family is not without expertise in creating five-star luxury from the proverbial sow's ear. They also own the Elora Mill in nearby Elora, long a hallmark of accommodation and culinary excellence in Canada.

Rooms at the Queen's have touchtone telephones, color TV, hair dryers, individual climate control and desk and chair. There are three sizes of suites. Those on the top floor have skylights and two bathrooms. The sitting rooms have loveseats that pull out into beds.

One Stratford tradition was maintained by creating the Edinburgh Room, an intimate dining room, and another tradition was imported from St. Catharines by the Taylor family. The Edinburgh Room was transformed from the Edinburgh Lounge. Before the Taylors bought the hotel the lounge was a hangout whose habitués favored wearing ball caps while dining. The room is named after the Duke of Edinburgh who, during a royal visit to the Stratford Festival in 1959, complained publicly about Stratford's archaic liquor laws.

The imported tradition is the Taylor and Bate Ltd. Brewing Pub, a popular spot with locals and tourists alike. A brewery by that name was founded in St. Catharines in 1837 by the great-great-grandfather of the present inn owner, Crozier Taylor. That brewery was bought out in 1935, but Taylor has brought it all back to life again in Stratford.

It's a pine-paneled pub where draft beer is brewed and served. Patrons can feel comfortable in jeans and sip at their stein or highball on bar chairs or around circular pine tables.

Next to the 40-seat Edinburgh Room is the Pinkney Dining Room in pink and gray decor, and across the lobby is a bright, pleasant lounge. Tinkling music from a white baby grand piano entertains guests from breakfast through evening.

Menu choices at the Queen's Inn are limited but appealing and change frequently, with offerings inspired by the produce of the season. Here is one recipe that has proven very popular with guests.

Queen's Inn Steak and Lager Stew
(Serves 4-6)

2 lbs stewing beef, in 1-inch cubes
4 T olive oil
2 medium onions, thinly sliced
2 cloves garlic, finely chopped
4 T tomato paste
1/2 cup flour
1 bottle domestic beer
4 cups beef stock

1 16-oz can tomatoes
1 bay leaf
Pinch of thyme
Salt and freshly ground pepper to taste
1 carrot, diced
1 stick celery, diced
1/4 lb fresh mushrooms, sliced

Sear the beef cubes in a hot frying pan. Drain in a colander, keeping the juices. Heat olive oil in a large pot and sweat the onions until they are translucent. Add finely chopped garlic and the beef cubes. Add tomato paste and flour and stir until meat is well coated. Stir in beer, beef stock, the can of tomatoes (including the juice) and the reserved meat juices. Add the bay leaf, thyme and salt and pepper; let simmer for 1 hour. Add carrot, celery and mushrooms; simmer for 30 minutes. Serve the stew on a bed of rice or with fresh hot rolls.

Glen Roberts Tea Room and Steak House

Fine home-style cooking for lunch and dinner in a rustic 1898 one-room school house decorated with a large collection of Canadian antiques.

Innkeepers:	Tom and Peggy Ludlow
Address:	Glen Roberts Dr., Trout Creek, Ont. P0H 2L0
Telephone:	705-723-5327
Rooms:	No accommodation
Children:	Yes
Open:	Year round. Tues.–Sat. Lunch and afternoon tea noon–2; Dinner 6–11. Reservations required for dinner
Food rates:	Lunch $$; Dinner $$$
Smoking:	No restrictions; smoke-free areas
Dress code:	Informal
Facilities:	Fully licensed; two dining areas; play area for children; pleasant walking trail; flower and herb gardens
Attractions:	Art and craft studio on premises; Commanda General Store and Museum is 21 km (13 miles) west of Trout Creek on Highway 522
Wheelchairs:	Not accessible
Directions:	3 km (2 miles) south of Trout Creek, turn west on Glen Roberts Dr.

In winter it's cozy around the wood stove in what used to be the basement of the old Glen Roberts school. In summer you might want to have lunch upstairs in what was the school's only classroom, admiring the magnificent collection of antiques and looking out at the carefully tended flower gardens.

The school was closed in 1966 and stood empty until Tom found it for sale in 1974. He had come north to go canoeing, but when that was rained out he went looking at country property listings. He and Peggy renovated the building and opened an antique shop and tea room the following spring.

Later they started serving home-style North American dinners — surf and turf, lobster tails, pickerel, stuffed fillet of sole, spare ribs, pork, lamb and steaks. All the herbs are grown on the property, and in season the gardens provide all the vegetables and salad ingredients.

Out back Tom is gradually re-creating the entire village of Glen Roberts, which, when he and Peggy arrived, consisted of only the old school house. The village homes and shops had been reclaimed by the bush from which they had been so painstakingly hacked well over a century ago. An old stockade and other structures are designed as play areas for visiting children.

There's a limited selection for lunches — usually a soup of the day, a couple of entrees and desserts, all accompanied with buttermilk scones and homemade preserves, some of which may also be bought in the upstairs antiques and gift shop areas.

Peggy has kindly shared the recipe for one of her popular chutneys, a smashing accompaniment to chicken, pork or fish.

Glen Roberts Rhubarb Chutney

2 lbs finely chopped rhubarb
1 lb sultana raisins
2 lbs white or *brown sugar*
1 large lemon, finely chopped
1 pint vinegar
1/2 t cayenne
1 oz bruised gingerroot, chopped

Combine all ingredients in a large kettle and boil until thick. Ladle into sterilized jars and seal.

The Hartley House

Down-home informality, good home-style cooking and lots of it, with friendly service in one of a vanishing breed of small-town downtown hotels.

Innkeepers:	Lorne, Dave and Chris Schmalz
Address:	130 Durham St., P.O. Box 790, Walkerton, Ont. N0G 2V0
Telephone:	519-881-1040
Rooms:	34 rooms all with bathroom en suite
Children:	Yes
Pets:	No
Open:	Year round, daily. Dining room: Mon.–Fri. 10:30–2, 5–9; Sat. 11–2, 4:30–9:30; Sun. 9–2, 4:30–8
Room rates:	$
Food rates:	Lunch $; Dinner $$
Smoking:	No restrictions
Dress code:	Informal
Facilities:	Fully licensed dining room; bar/lounge; bowling alley; pool tables; shuffleboard; newsstand/gift shop
Attractions:	Small-town ambience; near golf courses; antique shops; the Saugeen River; Blyth Festival
Wheelchairs:	Public rooms accessible; guest rooms not accessible
Directions:	On the main street at main intersection, Durham (Highway 4) and Jackson streets

The three-story Hartley House hotel has anchored the main intersection in the town of 4,500 since 1860. A Niagara of beer has flowed through its saloon taps during that time, and the business and political deals cooked up in its back rooms probably total in the hundreds of millions of dollars by now.

Since it opened, the hotel has had only three owners. Lorne Schmalz bought it in 1939 and runs it with his son, Dave, and Dave's wife, Chris. The hotel may not have any stars with its listing in the Ontario accommodations guide, but it has received a number of awards, including one for warmest hospitality.

The guest rooms vary in size and layout, and most are large and have two double beds. Each room has a TV, and air conditioning with a window unit whose motor drowns out the night sounds of a small town and eventually lulls you to sleep. The furniture is early miscellaneous, but everything works and two people can get a room for four or five nights for the price of one night in an average room in Toronto or Ottawa.

The region's social center is the warren of bars and lounges and games rooms on the hotel's first floor. There's even a full-size bowling alley with pool tables. The local clientele is friendly; they're happy to tell you what fish are biting where and at what, the level of the Saugeen River if you're planning to canoe it, and when the slowest times are on the local golf courses.

The large lobby of the Hartley House is a museum to a happier, more relaxed era fast fading from rural Canada. There you can buy a bus ticket, a good cigar or a plug of chewing tobacco. You can get mix and ice for that nightcap in your room, candy bars or a dozen different newspapers. There are magazines and paperbacks, toothpaste and headache tablets, and always someone with the time to give you directions or tell you about some local point of interest.

The hotel has built a fine reputation over the years for its smorgasbord dinners, Sunday brunches and Bruce County beef. The feasts are held in the 60-seat dining room still decorated with the original basswood paneling, wood that has bounced back well over a century of service club and political rhetoric.

Sunday brunches often find a bizarre mix of clientele seated at adjoining tables: at one there may be two or three generations doing the monthly duty lunch with great-grandmother, all of them uncomfortable on a warm summer's day in shirts and ties and fussy dresses.

At the next table, yuppies weekending away from the city may be clad in fluorescent shorts on their way to or from canoeing or fishing the river.

Steve Richard, the hotel's executive chef, has a background of many years at Toronto's Windsor Arms Hotel, known for its exceptional cuisine. Steve offers the following recipe.

Hartley House Pork Tenderloin

(Serves 4)

2 pork tenderloins
Salt and black pepper to taste
1/2 oz vegetable oil
2 oz port
1 t ground sage

2 oz butter
1 large yellow apple, cored and sliced
1 cup demiglace or gravy
2 oz crushed hazelnuts

Cut each tenderloin into 6 portions and flatten to scallopini size. Season with salt and pepper. Brown in vegetable oil in a hot frying pan for 1 1/2 to 2 minutes. Remove from pan and place on a warming plate. Pour off oil from pan; add port and ground sage. Boil away half of the port. Add butter and apple slices; lightly poach. Add demiglace or gravy; bring to a boil. Add tenderloins to sauce, garnish with crushed hazelnuts, and reheat 2–3 minutes.

Cavanagh's Olde Stone House

The 1880 graystone Williamsford General Store has been convincingly converted to a country-style inn where guests can enjoy fine dining including some unique dishes.

Innkeepers:	Elizabeth and Bob (The Squire) Cavanagh
Address:	General Delivery, Williamsford, Ont. N0H 2V0
Telephone:	519-794-2622
Rooms:	No accommodation
Children:	Yes
Open:	Year round daily except Tuesdays. Lunch noon–2:30; Dinner 5–10.
Food rates:	Lunch $; Dinner $$
Smoking:	No pipes or cigars in dining room
Dress code:	Casual
Attractions:	In the heart of Grey-Bruce counties, surrounded by cross-country ski trails, antique shops and scenic country backroads ideal for viewing autumn foliage
Wheelchairs:	Dining room and washrooms accessible
Directions:	On Highway 6 in Williamsford, between Durham and Owen Sound

Cavanagh's Olde Stone House is comfortable and homey, unpretentious and relaxing, and the antiques that adorn the walls of this former general store — bottles, plates, bells, pitchers and other bits and pieces on the plate rail which rings the single dining room —

don't scream to be noticed, and nor do the framed pictures and stained glass windows. The decor is as refreshingly subtle and restrained as the background music and makes the visitor feel utterly at ease. There's a lovely and well-stocked antique bar and the original wooden floors, and a glass-doored wood stove spices the air when its door is opened in cold weather to admit another log.

The inn has a thoroughly researched wine list to complement the menu and offers monthly gourmet dinners on various themes. The meals are usually five or six courses and accompanied by three or more suitable wines, which are included in the modest prix fixe charge.

The lunch offerings are light, with a daily soup and sandwich choice, tossed or Caesar salad and entrees such as crab cheese melt, fettuccini primavera and seafood crêpe. The lunch and dinner menus change quarterly to take advantage of seasonal fruits, vegetables and meats, and "from time to time" there are daily specials in addition to the fish plate of the day.

The dinner menu often offers rabbit; one of the Squire's recipes is more than a century old and calls for the rabbit to be cooked in mustard and a gin sauce. There's yet a different treatment in the following recipe.

Cavanagh's Rabbit Dijonnaise

(Serves 4)

1 t salt	1 cup beef stock
1/4 t freshly ground green peppercorns	2 oz brandy
1 t tarragon	3 T flour
1 T Dijon mustard	6 T cold water
1 rabbit, about 4 lbs, cut in 12 pieces	1 T Dijon mustard
2 T butter	1 T chopped fresh parsley
2 T virgin olive oil	

Blend salt, pepper, tarragon and 1 T mustard, and brush on both sides of the rabbit pieces. Melt butter in heavy skillet; add oil, and brown rabbit. Add beef stock and brandy; cover and simmer over low heat for about 1 hour. Remove rabbit to platter and keep warm. Pour 1 cup of cooking juices into small saucepan. Thoroughly blend flour and cold water, and stir into saucepan, cooking over medium heat until thickened. Stir in 1 T mustard and pour over rabbit immediately before serving. Garnish with chopped parsley.

The General Wolfe Hotel

A modern-looking historic inn with 7 guest rooms overlooking Kingston from Wolfe Island, a short ferry trip away. Continental cuisine, exceptional service.

Innkeepers:	Hana and Miroslav Zborovsky
Address:	P.O. Box 100, Wolfe Island, Ont. K0H 2Y0
Telephone:	613-385-2611
Rooms:	7 rooms all with bathroom en suite
Children:	Yes
Pets:	Yes
Open:	Year round, 5:30–2. Closed Mondays in winter
Room rates:	$
Food rates:	Lunch $; Dinner $$
Smoking:	No pipes or cigars in dining room; smoking areas available
Dress code:	Casual
Facilities:	Three dining rooms and bar/lounge; free docking for hotel patrons at marina across the street
Attractions:	A short ferry trip from Kingston's many attractions: Old Fort Henry; boat tours; Marine Museum; Agnes Etherington Art Centre; Bellevue House; historic City Hall; Maclachlan Woodworking Museum; Royal Military College Museum; Pump House Steam Museum
Wheelchairs:	All public rooms accessible; guest rooms not accessible
Directions:	In Marysville one block from the ferry dock

When the owner works for fun and has created the menu from his own experiences, you can usually count on a memorable dining experience. At The General Wolfe Hotel you can add a great view to the equation, whether you're dining at high noon or watching old Sol slip below the horizon, spilling a paletteful of glossy hues across the waters of the St. Lawrence River.

The General Wolfe was built as a hotel in 1853, but it was modernized in 1987 and shows no sign of its age. Large plate glass picture windows overlook the St. Lawrence River, and the long, rambling building is sheathed in cedar siding. The guest rooms are of different sizes and configurations and all are air-conditioned.

Inside, the dining rooms are inviting with linen tablecloths, comfortable furniture and a lot of service going on at your tableside. Salads are built there, some steaks and crêpes are flambéed there and dishes like Chateaubriand are sliced and served at the table.

The lunch menu has four appetizers, four soups and four salads. The eight entrees include halibut, scallops and fillet of sole. There are two steaks, Hungarian goulash, a lamb shishkebab and curried Bombay chicken.

The choice expands enormously for dinner, when the special is a gourmet dinner with choice of steak, lamb, fish or pheasant for the entree. The rack of lamb is broiled in a herb mustard with pistachios; the pheasant is deglazed with a burgundy sauce.

Wolfe Island is at the point where the St. Lawrence River starts emptying Lake Ontario. It's low and flat, with quiet farms and peaceful rural roads wandering through woods and meadows. The island is reached by ferry from downtown Kingston, year-round. It's a 20-minute trip each way and there's no charge for passengers or vehicles. There are frequent sailings in summer and fewer in the other seasons.

The Zborovskys fled their native Czechoslovakia for Vienna in 1968 as Soviet tanks rolled across the border, and 10 days later they were in Toronto, seeking political asylum. In just over a year Miroslav owned his own restaurant in Toronto but within a decade moved to the more peaceful setting of Wolfe Island.

"I don't work here," Miroslav explained of his restaurant. "I come here to have fun. It's like having a dinner party for our friends every night." While Miroslav oversees the dining rooms, Hana supervises a staff of eight chefs in the kitchen, from which this recipe came.

General Wolfe Crêpes Suzette
(Serves 4)

Crêpes

1/2 cup half & half cream
1/2 oz brandy
2 eggs
3 T all purpose flour
Grated rind of 1/2 lemon
Pinch of salt

Sauce

8 T granulated sugar
2 T butter
2 T brandy
Juice of 1 lemon
1 orange, halved
1 lemon, halved
2 T Grand Marnier
8 scoops vanilla ice cream
2 T toasted almonds for garnish (optional)

To make crêpes: Mix all ingredients. Lightly oil a moderately heated pan. Pour paper-thin layer of batter into pan. Cook both sides until the crêpe appears dry. Remove from pan and keep warm.

To make sauce: Heat a heavy skillet over high heat. Arrange a ring of sugar in skillet, place butter in center and cook until the mixture starts to caramelize; *do not allow it to brown.* Flame with brandy. Add lemon juice and orange and lemon halves, cut side down. Rub the fruits against the bottom of the pan to prevent sticking and to release some of the juice. Simmer until sauce separates. Remove fruit halves.

Place crêpes in the sauce one at a time and fold into sauce from both sides. Flambé with Grand Marnier and serve over vanilla ice cream. Spoon remaining sauce over crêpes. Sprinkle with toasted almond slices, if desired.

Hessenland Country Inn

A family restaurant specializing in German dishes, with 13 motel-style units and, on summer weekends, a German beer garden with dance floor.

Innkeepers:	Ernst and Christa Ihrig
Address:	R.R. 2, Zurich, Ont. N0M 2T0
Telephone:	519-236-7707
Rooms:	12 motel-type units; one two-story honeymoon suite (one-bedroom apartment with kitchenette)
Children:	Yes
Pets:	No
Open:	Year round. Lunch 11–2; Dinner 6–9; Sunday brunch 11–2:30
Room rates:	$$. Midweek and weekend packages available
Food rates:	Lunch $; Dinner $$
Smoking:	No restrictions; smoke-free area available
Dress code:	Informal
Facilities:	Fully licensed dining room and beer garden; outdoor heated pool; short walk from beach on Lake Huron; windsurfing; pony rides; cross-country skiing; horse-drawn sleigh rides
Attractions:	Near Blyth Festival; Huron Country Playhouse; Zurich Bean Festival; attractions of Grand Bend, Bayfield and Goderich
Wheelchairs:	All areas accessible
Directions:	On Highway 21 midway between Grand Bend and Bayfield

Hessenland is a newcomer to Ontario's country inns but already has a loyal following of folks from the surrounding area and nearby Michigan who enjoy good German-style food and a beer garden with oom-pah band. Ernst and Christa opened a restaurant specializing in German food in 1984. The following season they added 12 motel units and a two-story honeymoon suite. The decor of the rooms, hallways and dining room is white stucco with dark wooden beams.

The double motel units each have two queen-size beds, a table and two comfortable chairs, color TV and a small refrigerator. There's a vanity and basin with well-lighted makeup mirror outside the three-piece bathroom. The single units each have one queen-size bed and a studio couch that can pull out into a double bed.

The honeymoon unit has the bedroom on the ground floor with a whirlpool bath for two and a canopied bed complete with colored lights that reflect off a rotating mirror ball under the canopy. Upstairs is a large living room with a view over the surrounding farm country and Lake Huron. You don't have to be honeymooning to rent the suite, but you do have to book it well in advance because it has become a popular weekend hideaway.

Low dividers separate the large dining room into four areas, increasing the feeling of privacy. Most dishes are German — schnitzels, rouladen, wurstplatte, sauerbraten — but there is also fresh fish, shrimp tempura, pork, steaks and chicken and there are a few items especially for children. One of the most popular dishes is the Hessenland platter for two, on which the chef arranges a selection from the daily menu.

On Friday and Saturday nights when the beer garden is in full swing, tour companies bring in bus loads of revelers from Ontario and Michigan to sing and dance and attack a full German buffet dinner. Hessenland's recipe for one of their more popular menu offerings follows.

Hessenland Beef Gulasch

(Serves 4)

1/2 cup lard
2 lbs beef shoulder, diced
2 lbs onions, chopped
2 cloves garlic, chopped
3 t paprika
1 t salt
1/2 t pepper
4 cups water
2 green peppers, diced
2 sweet red peppers, diced
2 T cornstarch
2 T sour cream (optional)

Heat lard to high temperature in a roasting pan. Add diced beef and brown on all sides. Add chopped onions and continue cooking until they are golden brown. Stir in garlic, paprika and salt and pepper. Add water. Reduce heat and let simmer for 1 1/2–2 hours. Add diced peppers and cook for 15 minutes. In a measuring cup, dissolve cornstarch in a little water; add paste to stew to thicken. If desired, add sour cream before serving. Serve with homemade noodles or dumplings.

Alphabetical Index of Inns

Albion Hotel (The), Bayfield 15
Ancaster Old Mill Inn, Ancaster 12
Angeline's Restaurant/Bloomfield Inn, Bloomfield 23
André's Swiss Country Dining, Port Elgin 114
Beachburg Inn, Beachburg 21
Benjamin's Inn, St. Jacobs 132
Benmiller Inn, Benmiller 61
Brickyard (The), Sault Ste. Marie 122
Café 13, Cambridge 32
Cataract Inn, Cataract 4
Cavanagh's Olde Stone House, Williamsford 155
Cesira's Italian Cuisine, Sault Ste. Marie 124
Chantry House Inn, Southampton 138
Chequers (The), Stittsville 144
Courtyard Restaurant, Ottawa 106
Ducks on the Roof, Amherstburg 10
Elm Hurst, Ingersoll 78
Elora Mill Country Inn, Elora 53
Emo Inn, Emo 56
Emporium (The Great British), New Dundee 92
Erie Beach Hotel, Port Dover 111
Fisherman's Wharf Restaurant and Motel, Meaford 86
Frenchman's Inn Restaurant, Exeter 58
General Wolfe Hotel (The), Wolfe Island 157
Glen Roberts Tearoom and Steakhouse, Trout Creek 150
Grandview Inn, Huntsville 72
Hartley House (The), Walkerton 152
Herigate Inn, Milton 88
Heritage Inn (The), Mount Pleasant 90

Hessenland, Zurich 160
Hotel Bedford (The), Goderich 64
Hudson House, Combermere 46
Inn at the Falls, Bracebridge 29
Kettle Creek Inn (The), Port Stanley 116
La Brassine, Goderich 67
Langdon Hall, Cambridge 35
Little Inn (The), Bayfield 18
Millcroft Inn, Alton 7
Maples (The), Bloomfield 26
Mrs. Mitchell's, Violet Hill 129
Norsemen Restaurant, Huntsville 75
Nottawasaga Inn, Alliston 1
Oban Inn, Niagara-on-the-Lake 98
Olde Heidelberg Brewery and Restaurant, Heidelberg 70
Opinicon (The), Chaffey's Locks 38
Pelee Island Hotel, Pelee Island 109
Prince of Wales Hotel (The), Niagara-on-the-Lake 101
Queen's Inn (The), Kingston 81
Queen's Inn at Stratford (The), Stratford 147
Riverview Lodge (The), Dryden 48
Rossport Inn, Rossport 119
Rockgarden Terrace Resort, Spring Bay 141
Severn River Inn, Severn Bridge 126
Spike and Spoon (The), Collingwood 44
Teddy Bear Bed and Breakfast Inn, Elmira 50
Traditions, North Bay 104
Unicorn Inn (The), South Gillies 135
Walper Terrace Hotel, Kitchener 83
Waterlot (The), New Hamburg 95
Woodlawn Terrace Inn, Cobourg 41

Index of Recipes

SALADS
Caesar 55
Spinach salad 85

APPETIZERS
Chicken liver pâté 11
Chicken liver pâté 60
Goat cheese mousseline 37

ENTREES
Beef Gulasch 162
Beef Stroganoff 52
Chicken, basil 123
Chicken, cordon rouge 105
Chicken Grand Marnier 74
Chicken, herbed fromage 80
Chicken, Provençal 69
Chicken, tarragon 89
Chile con carne 82
Crab and shrimp crêpes 87
Fettuccini Alfredo 125
Fettuccini Victoria 43
Lamb, roast rack 91
Pasta Portofino 66
Pepper steak 57
Pickerel, pan fried 110
Pickerel paupiettes 20
Pig tails 71
Pork tenderloin 154
Rabbit Dijonnaise 156
Rabbit Morengo 97
Salmon, baked Atlantic 103
Seafood Costa Brava 146
Seafood lasagna 17
Shrimp and scallop sauté 118
Steak and kidney pie 31
Steak and lager stew 149
Sweet potato pancakes 134
Torta rustica 128
Trois filet teriyaki 34
Trout Hemingway 121
Veal cutlets Viennese 143
Veal medallions 49
Veal shank, braised 9
Veal Zurichoise 115

DESSERTS
Cactus pear sherbet 137
Chocolate mousse 3
Chocolate pie 22
Chocolate truffle pie 47
Crêpes Suzette 159
Raspberry/chocolate cheesecake 25
Raspberry cottage cake 108
Raspberry soufflé 6
Rhubarb pie 40
Rum pot 28

RELISHES
Cranberry vinaigrette 77
King Edward VII sauce 100
Pear mint chutney 45
Pickled pumpkin 113
Rhubarb chutney 151

BREADS
Cream puffs, Mennonite 140
Sage bread 63
Scones 94
Spoon bread 131
Whole wheat bread 14